RELIGIOUS EXPERIENCING

William James
and
Eugene Gendlin

John J. Shea

UNIVERSITY
PRESS OF
AMERICA

LANHAM • NEW YORK • LONDON

Library of Congress Cataloging-in-Publication Data

Shea, John J., 1940-
  Religious experiencing.

  Bibliography: p.
  1. James, William, 1842-1910—Contributions in
interpretation or religious experience. 2. Gendlin,
Eugene T., 1926-   —Contributions in interpretation
of religious experience. 3. Experience (Religion)—
History. I. Title.
BL53.S49   1987   291.4'2   86-33957
ISBN 0-8191-6136-5 (alk. paper)
ISBN 0-8191-6137-3 (pbk. : alk. paper)

All University Press of America books are produced on acid-free
paper which exceeds the minimum standards set by the National
Historical Publication and Records Commission.

Acknowledgements

I want to express my deep gratitude to:

Eugene T. Gendlin, Ph.D., for sharing his "experiencing."

Rev. Peter A. Campbell, Ph.D., and Rev. Edwin M. McMahon, Ph.D., for their insights and support when this book was becoming a dissertation.

Rev. Neil J. McGettigan, O.S.A., for his expert editorial assistance.

James J. Shea, for his invaluable help with word processing.

The Augustinian Community of Merrimack College, North Andover, Massachusetts, for their hospitality during the academic year of 1985-1986.

I am also grateful to the following for their permission to use copyrighted material:

William James, The Varieties of Religious Experience, 1985, and The Principles of Psychology, Vol. I, 1983, Harvard University Press, Cambridge, Massachusetts. Reprinted by permission.

The William James Archives, Houghton Library, Harvard University, Cambridge, Massachusetts, for brief quotations. By permission of the Houghton Library.

From Experiencing and the Creation of Meaning: A Philosophical and Psychological Approach to the Subjective by Eugene T. Gendlin. Copyright 1962 by The Free Press, a division of Macmillan, Inc. Reprinted by permission of the publisher.

F. E. Peacock Publishers, Inc., for permission to quote from Current Psychotherapies, First and Second Editions, Raymond Corsini, ed., 1973, 1979.

TABLE OF CONTENTS

INTRODUCTION

"The place to look is all places, the place to stand is no place at all."[1]

This book is about religion in its immediacy, in its livingness. It offers a re-visioning of the role of "feeling" in religious experience by looking at an actual phenomenon, the process of "religious experiencing."

Since the time of Schleiermacher, "feeling" has had a prominent place in the literature of religion. Many religious thinkers have struggled with it, seeing it as somehow being at the heart of religious experience, as somehow being the matrix out of which various religious concepts and creeds arise. In psychology as well, especially in some of the more recent psychotherapies, "feeling" has become an operative concept both in theory and in practice. This book, on the boundary between religion and psychology, draws from both disciplines in order to locate and to describe a process understanding of "religious feeling" or "religious experiencing."

The way I want to work toward a description of "religious experiencing" is through the thinking of two very gifted phenomenologists of feeling. One is William James, and the other is Eugene Gendlin. William James is, of course, well-known as a philosopher, psychologist, and religious thinker who wrote at the turn of the Century. In _The Varieties of Religious Experience_, he consistently relies on the concept of "feeling" to describe what is primary and alive in religious experience. In the _Varieties_, and especially in some of his other writings, he also finds an intrinsic connection between feeling and a process of change, or, in his terms, a process of "conversion" or "unification." Although he does not articulate clearly this connection between feeling and transformation, his need to be radically empirical and his genius for description combine to produce an inchoate understanding of feeling as a process, an understanding which has great heuristic value.

Eugene Gendlin, a philosopher, psychologist, and psychotherapist presently at the University of Chicago, wrestles with practical, growth-related questions, such as: How do people actually change? How can the process of therapeutic transformation be best described and facilitated? In addressing these questions, Gendlin elaborates his notion of "experiencing," that is, an understanding of the person in terms of pre-verbal, bodily-felt aliveness which, when directly attended to, can open up and change. Even though Gendlin says little on the role of "experiencing" in religion, his description of this "experiencing" is so foundational that it includes any kind or aspect of a person's experience, including the religious. His thinking makes it possible to focus on "religious experiencing" as part of a person's felt relatedness to reality. In other words, in the thinking of Gendlin there is a "place to look" for an understanding of religion as a process.

This book is also on the boundary between theory and practice. With the resources available in James and Gendlin, it offers, in terms of theory, a way of describing "religious experiencing" as a process of bodily-felt-relating to the divine. At the same time, it suggests practical implications of this phenomenon, especially in terms of religious counseling and religious education.

Chapter I, "William James: The Role of Feeling in Religious Experience," begins with a brief look at James's own sense of religious experience in relation to the writing of the Varieties. Next, it explores the characteristics of "feeling" described in the Varieties to see how this "feeling" functions in religion. Then, it looks at some of his other writings to see how he connects feeling with a sense of process. The chapter concludes with some critical reflections.

Chapter II, "Eugene Gendlin: The Experiencing Process," is a comprehensive presentation of Gendlin's "experiencing" or "feeling." First, it presents a basic definition of experiencing. Next, it describes experiencing as an interpersonal process of therapeutic change and growth. Then, it explores some further characteristics of experiencing, which are helpful for seeing religion as an ongoing process of the person. The chapter concludes with some critical reflections.

Chapter III, "A Process of Religious Experiencing," presents a fourfold description of the basic aspects of "religious experiencing" as this description is drawn from the thinking of James and Gendlin. Then, it views "religious experiencing" as inherently a process of change and growth. Finally, after pointing out some implications of "religious experiencing" for an understanding of experiential religion, it offers some shifts in perspective on religious education, pastoral counseling, and spiritual direction.

_____

ENDNOTE

1 Paul Tillich, <u>Systematic Theology</u>, Vol. I, New York, Harper & Row, 1967, p. 26.

CHAPTER ONE

WILLIAM JAMES:

THE ROLE OF FEELING IN RELIGIOUS EXPERIENCE

William James is aware, much like theologians Friedrich Schleiermacher and Rudolf Otto, of how central "feeling" is in an articulation of religious experience as a living phenomenon.[1] And long before the notion of "process" had any general acceptance in psychological thought, James realized that there is a definite connection between feeling and the process of change within the person. Although hampered by a somewhat static notion of "feeling," (at least in the Varieties of Religious Experience) his desire to approach feeling as phenomenologically as possible reveals insights into its nature which are invaluable.[2] His grapplings with religious feeling are the grapplings of a man who has both a need to understand and a genius for description. Much of Eugene Gendlin's "experiencing" process described in the next chapter will be viewed as a furthering of James's pioneering efforts.

1. James's Personal Religious Experience and the Varieties

This section looks at James's religious experience and at some of the personal factors which influenced the writing of the Varieties. James did have some religious feelings of his own. These feelings, neither as strong nor as pervasive as he would have wanted, he tried to comprehend more fully as he prepared the Gifford Lectures.[3]

1

a) James's Own Religious Experience

Perhaps the single most important influence on James was his father. In his last letter to his father who was dying, a letter written on December 14, 1982, he acknowledges his filial debt:

> All my intellectual life I derive from you; and though we have often seemed at odds in the expression thereof, I'm sure there's a harmony somewhere, and that our strivings will combine. What my debt to you is goes beyond all my powers of estimating,--so early, so penetrating and so constant has been the influence.[4]

There can be no doubt this influence was pervasive in the area of religion. His father was deeply and wholeheartedly religious, even though the form of this religion and its life in the family were hardly ordinary or institutional. What James found significant was not the particulars of his father's belief, but the life in him of that belief. As he said in the introduction to his father's _Literary Remains_,

> . . . the core and center of the thing in him was always interest and attitude, something realized at a stroke, and felt like a fire in his breast; and all attempts at articulate verbal formulation of it were makeshifts of a more or less desperately impotent kind.[5]

As Ralph Barton Perry comments on the kind of influence his father exerted on James: "It was the spirit and attitude that won him, rather than the doctrine--his father's piety, not his father's ideas."[6] While James could not adopt the mainly Swedenborgian tenets espoused by his father, the approach of his father to religion left some very definite traces in him. The substance of these traces is summed up well by Maurice Le Breton:

> . . . there is no denying that something of the elder James's abhorrence for eccle-

2

siasticisms of any kind, his individualism, his general freedom from outward show of piety, his optimistic tendencies, his interest in mystical experiences and even his idea of a "working, everyday God" has passed into William's thought and reappears from time to time in the son's writings, though mixed with and in a way corrected by, later, foreign elements.[7]

An account of a sustained period of depression that he suffered as a young man reveals James's own sense of religion. Writing in the guise of a French correspondent, he gives a long, vivid description of this experience in the <u>Varieties</u>, mentioning the role of religion in weathering the storm:

"Whilst in this state of philosophic pessimism and general depression of spirits about my prospects, I went one evening into a dressing-room in the twilight to procure some article that was there; when suddenly there fell upon me without any warning, just as if it had come out of the darkness, a horrible fear of my own existence. Simultaneously there arose in my mind the image of an epileptic patient whom I had seen in the asylum, a black-haired youth with greenish skin, entirely idiotic, who used to sit all day on one of the benches, or rather shelves against the wall, with his knees drawn up against his chin, and the coarse grey undershirt, which was his only garment, drawn over them inclosing his entire figure. He sat there like a sort of sculptured Egyptian cat or Peruvian mummy, moving nothing but his black eyes and looking absolutely non-human. This image and my fear entered into a species of combination with each other. <u>That shape am I</u>, I felt, potentially. Nothing that I possess can defend me against that fate, if the hour for it should strike for me as it struck for him. There was such a horror of him, and such a perception of my own merely momentary discrepancy from him, that it was as if something hitherto solid within my breast gave way entirely, and I became a mass of quivering fear. After this the universe was changed for me altogether. I awoke morning after morning with a horrible dread at the pit of my stomach, and with the sense of the insecurity of life that I never knew before, and that I have never felt since."[8]

A few lines later, he adds: "I have always felt that this experience of melancholia of mine had a religious bearing."[9] He explains:

"I mean that the fear was so invasive and powerful that if I had not clung to scripture-texts like 'The eternal is my refuge,' etc., 'Come unto me, all ye that labor and are heavy-laden,' etc., 'I am the resurrection and the life,' etc., I think I should have grown really insane."[10]

From this description it would appear that James had some elements of belief and some sense of dependence on a personal God. What brought him out of his long depression, however, was not so much a reliance on God as a decision that he made, while influenced by the writings of Renouvier, to "voluntarily cultivate the feeling of moral freedom."[11]

Confirming the somewhat distant sense of religion suggested above and professing it as a basic attitude, James writes a few years later, in 1876:

My attitude toward religion is one of deference rather than adoption. I see its place; I feel that there are times when everything else was to fail and that, or nothing, remain; and yet I behave as if I must leave it untouched until such times come, and I am drawn to it by sheer stress of weather.[12]

In a letter to Thomas Davidson, January 8, 1882, there is evidence of an important shift from a sense of a personal and sustaining God, slight though that was, to a sense of the need for God as an ideal for human life and activity. James remarks:

> It is a curious thing, this matter of God! I can sympathize perfectly with the most rabid hater of him and the idea of him when I think of the use that has been made of him in history and philosophy as a <u>starting-point</u>, or premise for grounding deductions. But as an ideal to attain and make probable, I find myself less and less able to do without him.[13]

Nearly twenty years later, in some memoranda for the Gifford Lectures, the shift to a more engaging and activating sense of God as an ideal seems to be consolidated, even though there is an attendant sense of loss.

> Life comes to me as expressive of result, as dramatically significant, as shot through with an ideality to which I am bound to be faithful. And yet I cannot find in myself a trace of personal religion in the sense, in which so many possess it, nor any live belief in a conscious spirit of the universe with whom I may hold communion. I used to have something like this, but it has gone, beyond the possibility of recall; and the difference is so distinct that it makes me realize how positive and definite a thing religion may be in one's life, especially at times of sickness or grave trial.[14]

The clearest, most considered, most nuanced position of James in his later life with regard to his own sense of living religion is in a letter to James Leuba, April 17, 1904.

> My personal position is simple. I have no living sense of commerce with God. I envy those who have, for I know the addition of such a sense would help me immensely. The Divine, for my <u>active</u> life, is limited to abstract concepts which, as ideals, interest

5

and determine me, but do so but faintly in comparison with what a feeling of God might effect, if I had one. It is largely a question of intensity, but differences of intensity may make one's whole center of energy shift. Now, although I am so devoid of _Gottesbewustsein_ in the directer and stronger sense, yet there is _something_ _in_ _me_ which _makes_ _response_ when I hear utterances made from that lead by others. I recognize the deeper voice. Something tells me, "thither lies truth"--and I am _sure_ it is not old theistic habits and prejudices of infancy. Those are Christian; and I have grown so out of Christianity that entanglement therewith on the part of a mystical utterance has to be abstracted from and overcome, before I can listen. Call this, if you like, my mystical _germ_. It is a very common germ. It creates the rank and file of believers.[15]

The "mystical germ" he mentions in this letter raises the question of whether or not James actually had any mystical experiences himself. In introducing the topic of mystical states in the _Varieties,_ he confesses: "my own constitution shuts me out from their enjoyment almost entirely, and I can speak of them only at second hand."[16] Speaking of mysticism a few pages later, he remarks: "to me the living sense of its reality only comes in the artificial mystic state of mind."[17] Although James did not feel his own mystical experience was "exceptionally extensive,"[18] clearly he was attracted to and intrigued by mystical states of consciousness.[19] This attraction led him to an experiment with nitrous oxide in which he found the highlight of the experience to be "the tremendously exciting sense of an intense metaphysical illumination.[20] Aside, however, from feeling he gained an insight into Hegelian philosophy, he did not seem that impressed by the over-all quality of the experience. On another occasion he tried peyote in order to expand consciousness, but this time the reward was only severe nausea.[21]

The clearest account that James gives of an expe-

6

rience which could be counted as expanded or mystical, and which had some influence on the _Varieties_, is in a letter to his wife of July 9, 1898, in which he describes a night spent in the Adirondack Mountains:

> I spent a good deal of it in the woods, where the streaming moonlight lit up things in a magical checkered play, and it seemed as if the Gods of all nature-mythologies were holding an indescribable meeting in my breast with the moral Gods of the inner life. The two kinds of Gods have nothing in common--the Edinburgh lectures made quite a hitch ahead. The intense significance of some sort, of the whole scene, if one could only _tell_ the significance; the intense inhuman remoteness of its inner life, and yet the intense _appeal_ of it; its everlasting freshness and its immemorial antiquity and decay; its utter Americanism, and every sort of patriotic sug- gestiveness, and you, and my relation to you part and parcel of it all, and beaten up with it, so that memory and sensation all whirled inexplicably together; it was indeed worth coming for, and worth repeating year by year, if repetition could only procure what in its nature I suppose must be all unplanned for and unexpected.[22]

The kind of intense, ineffable oneness described in this passage attests to the fact that James did experience mystical consciousness which, although more naturalistic than theistic, he himself saw as related in some way to religious experience. It is also true that those who knew James well credit him with more of a mystical sense than he credits himself. A colleague, George Santayana, calls him "a mystic, a mystic in love with life."[23] Another friend and philosopher, John Boodin, writes of him at the time of his death:

> Mystic he was to a very much greater extent than he gave himself credit for being, just because of his vivid sense of first hand values, of the living reality of the flow of life and its fluent transitions.[24]

These reflections of Santayana and Boodin, and especially the night in the Adirondacks, show in James a mystical sensitivity to nature and the rhythm of life which leaves him open to the specifically religious mysticism of others.

b) The Writing of the Varieties

With regard to the religious influence of his father, James writes to his wife on January 6, 1883, shortly after his father's death:

> You have one new function hereafter, or rather no so much a new function as a new intellectualization of an old one: you must not leave me till I understand a little more of the value and meaning of religion in Father's sense, in the mental life and destiny of man. It is not the one thing needful as he said. But it is needful with the rest. My friends leave it altogether out. I as his son (if for no other reason) must help it to its rights in their eyes. And for that reason I must learn to interpret it aright as I have never done, and you must help me.[25]

Many years later, as he gathered and reflected on the religious material for the Gifford Lectures provided by friends and colleagues, James found himself basically receptive to it. He records in private notes: "I, for one, reading all these autobiographies, do not feel free to deny authority of mystical experience of which they are so redolent. I cannot ignore all this unanimous tradition."[26] When it came time to actually conceptualize his view of the nature and importance of religious experience, James writes to his long-time confidant, Frances Morse, revealing what are perhaps the two central themes of the Varieties. In a letter of April 12, 1900, he explains:

> The problem I have set myself is a hard one: first, to defend (against the prejudices of my "class") "experience" against "philosophy" as being the real backbone of the

8

world's religious life--I mean prayer, guidance and all that sort of thing immediately
and privately felt, as against high and noble
general views of our destiny and the world's
meaning; and second, to make the hearer or
reader believe, what I myself invincibly do
believe, that, although the special manifestations of religion may have been absurd (I
mean its creeds and theories), yet the life
of it as a whole is mankind's most important
function. A task well-nigh impossible, I
fear, and in which I shall fail; but the
attempt is my religious act.[27]

As recorded by the Edinburgh paper, The Scotsman,
James told his audience in the first of the Gifford
Lectures, that "he had his own little flow of private
religious faith, be the same strong or weak, and was
interested in rescuing it from the snares of the
enemy."[28]

Perry sums up well the working relationship of
James's own religious feeling to his respect for the
religious feeling of others, especially as a balance is
achieved in the Varieties, when he says of James:

. . . he was interested in the justifica-
tion of religion. His interest was never an
external one, but was the interest of one who
felt religion and was concerned for it. He
wanted to save a place for his own generalized religious feelings, but above all did he
want to save a place for the more concrete
beliefs of those more intensely pious fellow
creatures with whom he sympathized.[29]

Attention must now be turned to a closer examina-
tion of religious feeling, especially as it explicates
the theme of "experience" against "philosophy" in the
Varieties.

2. The Phenomenology of Feeling in the Varieties

This section of the chapter is an investigation
into the definition and function of "feeling" in The

Varieties of Religious Experience. First, the basic characteristics of "feeling" are seen, as "feeling" is contrasted to "conceptualization" in religious experience. Next, the essential relation that James finds between religious feeling and the experience of the divine is explored. Then, the religious response, that is, the way the person feels in relation to the divine, is considered. Finally, the relation between "feeling" and a process of change is viewed as it exists in the Varieties.

a) Characteristics of Feeling in Religious Experience

The phenomenon in religion that James consistently wants to focus on is the living, concrete reality as it is experienced. At the end of the original paragraph he wrote to begin the Gifford Lectures, he focuses on the living fullness of individual religion, contrasting this fullness with the inadequacy of concepts to capture it:

> Religion is the very citadel of human life, and the pretension to translate adequately into spread-out conceptual terms a kind of experience in which intellect, feeling and will, all our consciousness and all our unconsciousness together melt in a kind of chemical fusion, would be particularly abhorrent. Let me say then with frankness at the outset, that I believe that no so-called philosophy of religion can possibly begin to be an adequate translation of what goes on in the single private man, as he livingly expresses himself in religious faith and act.[30]

What seems inherent in this focus on living religion and what gradually emerges as the Varieties unfolds is an understanding of "feeling" in contrast to the "conceptual" in religion. James describes this contrast in a number of ways. At one point he says: "I do believe that feeling is the deeper source of religion, and that philosophic and theological formulas are secondary products, like translations of a text into another tongue."[31] A few lines later he clarifies his meaning of "secondary products" when he says: "in a world in which no religious feeling had ever existed, I doubt whether any philosophic theology could ever have been framed."[32]

Earlier in the <u>Varieties,</u> in the chapter on "The Reality of the Unseen," James describes this contrast between feeling and the conceptual in terms of "dumb intuition" and "rationalism." He observes:

> . . . if we look on man's whole mental life as it exists, on the life of men that lies in them apart from their learning and science, and that they inwardly and privately follow, we have to confess that the part of it which rationalism can give an account is relatively superficial. It is the part that has the <u>prestige</u> undoubtedly, for it has the loquacity, it can challenge you for proofs, and chop logic, and put you down with words. But it will fail to convince or convert you all the same, if your dumb intuitions are opposed to its conclusions. If you have intuitions at all, they come from a deeper level of your nature than the loquacious level which rationalism inhabits.[33]

James continues in this vein, now contrasting "subconscious life" with "consciousness," as he says: "Your whole subconscious life, your impulses, your faith, your needs, your divinations, have prepared the premises, of which your consciousness now feels the weight of the result."[34] A few lines later he reiterates what he has been saying, now contrasting "feelings of reality" with "reason," and suggesting a working relationship between them:

> The truth is that in the metaphysical and religious sphere, articulate reasons are cogent for us only when our inarticulate feelings of reality have already been impressed in favor of the same conclusion. Then, indeed, our intuitions and our reason work together, and the great world-ruling

systems, like that of the Buddhist or of the Catholic philosophy, may grow up.[35]

Having given a nod, however, to their working relationship, James goes on to stress the primacy of feeling over the rational:

> Our impulsive belief is here always what sets up the original body of truth, and our philosophy is but its showy verbalized translation. The immediate assurance is the deep thing in us, the argument is but a surface exhibition. Instinct leads, intelligence does but follow. If a person feels the presence of a living God after the fashion shown by my quotations, your critical arguments, be they never so superior, will vainly set themselves to change his faith.[36]

In his chapter on "Philosophy," James pays more attention to the positive role of the conceptual in religion. He acknowledges that religious experience "spontaneously and inevitably engenders myths, superstitions, dogmas, creeds, and metaphysical theologies, and criticisms of one set of these by adherents of another."[37] He notes:

> We are thinking beings, and we cannot exclude the intellect from participating in any of our functions. Even in soliloquizing with ourselves, we construe our feelings intellectually. Both our personal ideals and our religious and metaphysical experiences must be interpreted congruously with the kind of scenery which our thinking mind inhabits. The philosophic climate of our time inevitably forces its own clothing on us. Moreover, we must exchange our feelings with one another, and in so doing we have to speak, and to use general and abstract verbal formulas. Conceptions and constructions are thus a necessary part of our religion; and as moderator amid the clash of hypotheses, and mediator among the criticisms on one man's constructions by another, philosophy will

12

always have much to do.[38]

These examples are more than sufficient to show
that a contrast between "feeling" and the "conceptual"
emerges from James's focus on living religion. And the
"feeling" described within this contrast is beginning
to reveal four interrelated characteristics: it has
primacy; it has the depth; it is fact and reality; and
it embodies truth and knowledge.

The Primacy of Feeling

The first characteristics of "feeling" is one
already alluded to, that is, feeling is primal and
foundational in religion. Whatever conceptualizations
take place, whatever philosophies or theologies
develop, they are "secondary processes," dependent upon
the primary feeling for their existence.[39] All intellectual operations are "interpretive and inductive
operations, operations after the fact, consequent upon
religious feeling, not coordinate with it, not independent of what it ascertains."[40] Religious feelings are
"primitive and unreflective," "private and dumb,"[41] yet
these feelings, along with conduct, are the "essence"
of religion and, in contrast to conceptualization, the
"more constant elements."[42] Perhaps because James
feels this view is a bit disconcerting, he remarks
almost apologetically:

> Please observe, however, that I do not say
> that it is <u>better</u> that the subconscious and
> the non-rational should thus hold primacy in
> the religious realm. I confine myself to
> simply pointing out that they do so hold it
> as a matter of fact."[43]

The Depth of Feeling

Another way that James articulates the primacy of
feeling over the conceptual is in terms of "depth." He
speaks of the conceptual level of religion as "superfi-
cial."[44] "The unreasoned and the immediate assurance
is the deep thing in us, the reasoned argument is but a
surface exhibition."[45] Also, as noted above, he
asserts: "I do believe that feeling is the deeper

13

source of religion, and that philosophic and theological formulas are secondary products."[46] In speaking of the conversion experiences of Bunyan and Tolstoy, he describes "<u>something</u> welling up in the inner reaches of their consciousness."[47] James relies heavily, in fact, on the "subconscious" as a way of describing and explaining how the process of conversion or unification takes place.

Feeling as Fact and Reality

Within the contrast of feeling to conceptualization, James often characterizes feeling as in some sense more immediately factual or real than the conceptual. He points out, for example:

> Conceptual processes can class facts, define them, interpret them; but they do not produce them, nor can they reproduce their individuality. There is always a <u>plus</u>, a <u>thisness</u>, which feeling alone can answer for.[48]

In discussing a possible science of religion, James feels that as a science it must draw from facts of personal experience.

> What religion reports, you must remember, always purports to be a fact of experience: the divine is actually present, religion says, and between it and ourselves relations of give and take are actual. If definite perceptions of fact like this cannot stand upon their own feet, surely abstract reasoning cannot give them the support they are in need of.[49]

James refers again to feeling and the factual in the "Conclusions" of the <u>Varieties,</u> as he describes what lies beneath the subject-object split of experience:

> A conscious field <u>plus</u> its object as felt or thought of <u>plus</u> an attitude toward the object <u>plus</u> the sense of a self to whom the

14

attitude belongs--such a concrete bit of personal experience may be a small bit, but it is a solid bit as long as it lasts; not hollow, not a mere abstract element of experience, such as the 'object' is when taken all alone. It is a _full_ fact, even though it be an insignificant fact; it is of the _kind_ to which all realities whatsoever must belong; the motor currents of the world run through the like of it; it is on the line connecting real events with real events.[50]

He continues, now explicitly in terms of feeling and its relation to concrete existence:

That unshakable feeling which each one of us has of the pinch of his individual destiny as he privately feels it rolling out on fortune's wheel may be disparaged for its egotism, may be sneered at as unscientific, but it is the one thing that fills up the measure of our concrete actuality, and any would-be existent that should lack such a feeling, or its analogue, would be a piece of reality only half made up.[51]

Reality runs through feeling. To describe reality without taking account of feeling is "like offering a printed bill of fare as the equivalent for a solid meal."[52] "Religion," says James, "makes no such blunder."[53] A few paragraphs later, reminding the reader why he focused on the individual person in religion, he returns again to "reality" in the contrast between feeling and the conceptual:

You see now why I have been so individualistic throughout these lectures, and why I have seemed so bent on rehabilitating the element of feeling in religion and subordinating its intellectual part. _Individuality is founded in feeling; and the recesses of feeling, the darker, blinder strata of character, are the only places in the world in which we catch real fact in the making_, and directly perceive how events happen, and

how work is actually done. Compared with
this world of living individualized feelings,
the world of generalized objects which the
intellect contemplates is without solidity or
life.[54] (Emphasis mine)

Feeling as Truth and Knowledge

Speaking of "feelings of reality," James observes:
"They are as convincing to those who have them as any
direct sensible experiences can be, and they are, as a
rule, much more convincing than results established by
mere logic ever are."[55] He says of these feelings
that,

> . . . if you have them, and have them at
> all strongly, the probability is that you
> cannot help regarding them as genuine percep-
> tions of truth, as revelations of a kind of
> reality which no adverse argument, however
> unanswerable by you in words, can expel from
> your belief.[56]

It is the "impulsive belief" which sets up "the
original body of truth."[57] Therefore, "the attempt to
demonstrate by purely intellectual processes the truth
of the deliverances of direct religious experience is
absolutely hopeless."[58]

> Philosophy lives in words, but truth and
> fact well up into our lives in ways that
> exceed verbal formulation. There is in the
> living act of perception always something
> that glimmers and twinkles and will not be
> caught, and for which reflection comes too
> late. No one knows this as well as the phi-
> losopher.[59]

Commenting on the workings of the subconscious,
James notes that the individual "absolutely knows" in a
way "truer than any logic-chopping rationalistic
talk."[60] In describing those who have experienced
self-surrender, he remarks: "With those who undergo it
in its fullness, no criticism avails to cast doubt on
its reality. They know; for they have actually felt

16

the higher powers, in giving up the tension of their personal will."[61]

James also finds mystical states, which are states of religious feeling, to be authoritative for those who report them:

> They are states of insight into the depths
> of truth unplumbed by the discursive intel-
> lect. They are illuminations, revelations,
> full of significance and importance, all
> inarticulate though they remain; and as a
> rule they carry with them a curious sense of
> authority for after-time.[62]

b) Feeling and the Religious Referent

Perhaps the best statement of James's approach to the religious referent in feeling is his now-famous definition of religion as "the feelings, acts, and experiences of individual men in their solitude, so far as they apprehend themselves to stand in relation to whatever they may consider the divine."[63]

The "divine" is to be understood broadly as "any object that is godlike, whether it be a concrete deity or not."[64] It is "a primal reality as the individual feels impelled to respond to solemnly and gravely."[65] What is important is that the divine is experienced as a felt reality:

> It is as if there were in the human con-
> sciousness a sense of reality, a feeling of
> objective presence, a perception of what we
> may call 'something there,' more deep and
> more general than any of the special and par-
> ticular 'senses' by which the current psy-
> chology supposes existent realities to be
> originally revealed.[66]

Most of the personal testimony James presents in the Varieties are experiences of a Christian God. In his running commentary between these accounts, James himself uses the phrases: "the divine," "God's presence," "unseen order," and especially, "ideal power" or

17

"higher power." Not much importance, however, is attached to a further description or elaboration of what the "higher power" is like. In fact, he contends that when we speak of the divine "we are dealing with a field of experience where there is not a single conception that can be sharply drawn."[67]

Things are more or less divine, states of mind are more or less religious, reactions are more or less total, but the boundaries are always misty, and it is everywhere a question of amount and degree. Nevertheless, at their extreme of development, there can never be any question as to what experiences are religious. The divinity of the object and the solemnity of the reaction are too well marked for doubt.[68]

Within the immediate experiencing of the divine there is a correlation between the reality of the "object" and the intensity of the response:

We may now lay it down as certain that in the distinctly religious sphere of experience, many persons (how many we cannot tell) possess the objects of their belief, not in the form of mere conceptions which their intellect accepts as true, but rather in the form of quasi-sensible realities directly apprehended. As his sense of the real presence of these objects fluctuates, so the believer alternates between warmth and coldness in his faith.[69]

Still, while there is a correlation between the sense of reality of the religious object and the feeling in response to it, there does not seem to be a correlation between the reality of the object and the ability to articulate what it is.

The sentiment of reality can indeed attach itself so strongly to our object of belief that our whole life is polarized through and through, so to speak, by its sense of the existence of the thing believed in, and yet

18

that thing, for purpose of definite description, can hardly be said to be present to our
mind at all.[70]

It is important to note that James's discussion of
the "object of belief" or the "higher power" originates
within experience. He is describing an _experiential_
object, a referent given in feeling. He is describing
a _felt_ datum and is careful not to equate this with an
object of _sense_ data.

c) The Felt Religious Response

Notwithstanding his insistence on the religious
object or referent as being an essential part of religious feeling, James's greater interest is in the feeling response itself or in how religious feelings are
felt. It is these feelings which he finds so attrac-
tive in themselves and so enhancing for life.[71]

To begin with, there does not seem to be any one
unique feeling characteristic of religion. Religious
feeling depends on the individual who is experiencing
and on what he or she experiences.

As concrete states of mind, made up of a
feeling plus a specific sort of object, religious emotions of course are psychic entities
distinguishable from other concrete emotions;
but there is no ground for assuming a simple
abstract 'religious emotion' to exist as a
distinct elementary mental affection by
itself, present in every religious experience
without exception.[72]

In line with his phenomenology of individual religious feeling, he adds:

As there thus seems to be no one elementary religious emotion, but only a common
storehouse of emotions upon which religious
objects may draw, so there might conceivably
also prove to be no one specific and essential kind of religious object, and no one
specific and essential kind of religious

act.[73]

Allowing that there is no one essential religious feeling, James says, nevertheless, that the most common religious feeling is happiness or joy. He finds happiness to be characteristic of the "healthy-minded" individual who "looks on all things and sees that they are good."[74] For this kind of person religion is from the outset an experience of "union with the divine" and happiness is "congenital and irreclaimable."[75] For the "sick soul," as well, that is, for the person who must radically transcend the evil of the world, "the more complex ways of experiencing religion are new manners of producing happiness."[76] For this latter individual there is a "supernatural kind of happiness, when the first gift of natural existence is unhappy, as it so often proves itself to be."[77]

On the feeling of happiness as _uniquely_ felt in religious experience, James quotes Hilty:

> "The near presence of God's spirit," says a Swiss writer, "may be experienced in its reality--indeed _only_ experienced. And the mark by which the spirit's existence and nearness are made irrefutably clear to those who have ever had the experience is the utterly incomparable _feeling_ _of_ _happiness_ which is connected with the nearness, and which is therefore not only a possible and altogether proper feeling for us to have here below, but is the best and most indisputable proof of God's reality . . ."[78]

In connection with the process of conversion James mentions other religious feelings: a "sense of higher control" which is often present;[79] a feeling of "assurance" and "joyous connection," which is immediate and intuitive and which brings with it a sense that "all is ultimately well with one,"[80] and a "sense of clean and beautiful newness within and without."[81]

Similar feelings are mentioned as characteristic of the state of saintliness. For example, flowing from the sense of God's presence are feelings of safety, of

20

inner security, and of love for mankind.[82] There are also feelings of peace, tenderness, charity, resignation, fortitude, and patience--all identified with the experience of the higher power, especially as saintliness mingles with the mystical in "reconciling, unifying states."[83]

In addition, James describes "spiritual emotions" connected with saintliness. These include:
     1. A feeling of being in a wider life than that of this world's selfish little interests; and a conviction, not merely intellectual, but as it were sensible, of the existence of an Ideal Power . . .
     2. A sense of the friendly continuity of the ideal power with our own life and a willing self-surrender to its control.
     3. An immense elation and freedom, as the outlines of the confining selfhood melt down.
     4. A shifting of the emotional centre towards loving and harmonious affections, towards 'yes, yes,' and away from 'no,' where the claims of the non-ego are concerned.[84]

All of these various feelings, which James is describing as a response to the divine, are being described, as well, within a process of conversion and as the end-state of a process of religious growth or, in his word, saintliness. Just how James understands feeling in relation to this process is the next consideration.

d) Feeling, Conversion, and the Process of Unification

Religious conversion is one species of a general process of unification, that is, a process of "remedying inner incompleteness and reducing inner discord" in order to bring about "firmness, stability and equilibrium."[85] James describes this process in terms of feeling. He adopts a "from-to" model in which the person starts "from" a state of melancholy or depression. This state is characterized by feelings of "mere passive joylessness and dreariness, discouragement, dejection, lack of taste and zest and spring."[86] The indi-

21

vidual may feel "self-mistrust and self-despair"[87] as well as "self-contempt."[88] Often he or she has a "feeling of inward vile and wrong,"[89] or, perhaps, has a sense of "panic fear" or a "grisly blood-freezing heart-palsifying sensation" of evil.[90]

What the person comes "to" in this process are the kinds of feelings mentioned above: a "rapturous sort of happiness,"[91] a sense of "second birth,"[92] a feeling that natural evil is "swallowed up in supernatural good."[93] For some there is the feeling that the self has "emerged into the smooth waters of inner unity and peace."[94] There is a sense of unification both inner and outer, a union within self and a union with God. In all this, notes James, it is certain that the process "brings a characteristic sort of relief; and never such extreme relief as when it is cast into the religious mould."[95]

Conversion and unification are also described by James in terms of "a native hardness" or a rigidity of self which "must break down and liquefy."[96] This easing or flowing is often achieved through self-surrender.

> Give up the feeling of responsibility, let go your hold, resign the core of your destiny to higher powers, be genuinely indifferent as to what becomes of it all, and you will find not only that you gain a perfect inward relief, but often also, in addition, the particular goods you sincerely thought you were renouncing.[97]

Perhaps there are some individuals who never are and maybe never could be converted. He suggests by way of explanation that this kind of person is "frozen," and yet he says that even late in life "some thaw, some release may take place . . . and the man's heart may soften and break into religious feeling."[98]

"Field of Consciousness" Model of Conversion

It is a thermal analogy together with a spatial one that goes to make up a major construct that James uses to explain the process of conversion. He proposes a <u>field</u> <u>of</u> <u>consciousness</u>. Within this field, there is a part or sub-field which "figures as focal and contains the excitement, and from which, as from a centre, the aim seems to be taken."[99]

Talking of this part, we involuntarily apply words of perspective to distinguish it from the rest, words like 'here,' 'this,' 'now,' 'mine,' or 'me'; and we ascribe to the other parts the positions 'there,' 'then,' 'that,' 'his' or 'thine,' 'it,' 'not me.' But a 'here' can change to a 'there,' and a 'there' become a 'here,' and what was 'mine' and what was 'not mine' change their places.[100]

James goes on, explaining:

What brings such changes about is the way in which emotional excitement alters. Things hot and vital to us to-day are cold to-morrow. It is as if seen from the hot parts of the field that the other parts appear to us, and from these hot parts personal desire and volition make their sallies. They are in short the centres of our dynamic energy, whereas the cold parts leave us indifferent and passive in proportion to their coldness.[101]

Applying this description to religion, he says:

. . . the focus of excitement and heat, the point of view from which the aim is taken, may come to lie permanently within a certain system; and then, if the change be a religious one, we call it a <u>conversion</u>, especially if it be by crisis, or sudden.[102]

How the excitement shifts and why aims that were peripheral become central can only be generally described by psychology; neither an outside observer nor the person having the experience can fully explain it.[103] "All we know is that there are dead feelings, dead ideas and cold beliefs, and there are hot and live ones, and when one grows hot and alive within us, everything has to re-crystalize about it."[104]

In elaborating other factors in the process of change, James mentions: "The collection of ideas alters by subtraction or by addition in the course of experience, and tendencies alter as the organism gets more aged."[105] "New information, however acquired, plays an accelerating part in the changes; and the slow mutation of our instincts and propensities, under the 'unimaginable touch of time,' has an enormous influence."[106] And "emotional occasions, especially violent ones, are extremely potent in precipitating mental rearrangements."[107]

"Subconscious" Model of Conversion

But as if still not satisfied with his explanation of change, James introduces what seems to be a second major construct to explain conversion and unification, a construct which centers around the subconscious as it breaks into consciousness. In contrasting the "voluntary" type of conversion to the way of "self-surrender," he sees that the voluntary or conscious approach to conversion is often insufficient to bring change about. Characteristically, this approach ends in "partial self-surrender" because, when the will has "done its uttermost towards bringing one close to the complete unification aspired after, it seems that the very last step must be left to other forces and performed without the help of its activity. In other words, self-surrender becomes then indispensable"[108]

To explain the "other forces" that must be relied on, James introduces, in an organismic way, the action of the "subconscious":

> A man's conscious wit and will, so far as they strain towards the ideal, are aiming at something only dimly and inaccurately imagined. Yet all the while the forces of mere organic ripening within him are going on towards their own prefigured result, and his conscious strainings are letting loose sub-

24

conscious allies behind the scenes, which in their way work towards rearrangement; the rearrangement towards which all these deeper forces tend is pretty surely definite, and definitely different from what he consciously conceives and determines.[109]

Relying on the work of his former pupil, Edwin Starbuck, James finds that "to exercise the personal will is still to live in the region where the imperfect self is the thing most emphasized."[110] When, however, "the subconscious forces take the lead, it is more probably the better self *in posse* which directs the operation."[111] The person seeking conversion must, in Starbuck's words, "fall back on the larger 'Power that makes for righteousness,' which has been welling up in his own being, and let it finish in its own way the work it has begun."[112]

3. James's Thinking on Experience, Feeling, and Process Other Than in the Varieties

As a way of further situating James's understanding of religious experience and as a way of throwing additional light on the role of "feeling" and its sense of process in the Varieties, some of James's other writings that were also inspired by a phenomenology of individual experience or feeling are briefly examined.

a) The Primacy of Experience

It is especially true for James that his general understanding of experience influences and is influenced by his understanding of religious experience. In fact, one reason he is so interested in experience is that he wants to do justice to all the various religious phenomena.[113] He works toward as inclusive an understanding of experience as possible; he wants to avoid reductionism simply because such an approach to experience is inadequate. As he stated in A Pluralistic Universe, published a few years after the Varieties: "I think it may be asserted that there are religious experiences of a specific nature, not deducible by analogy or psychological reasoning from other

25

sorts of experience."114

In focusing on any kind of experience, including the religious, James is interested in the fullness of its immediacy, that is, in the present living phenomenon before it is split by the subject-object dichotomy so operative in modern philosophy and science. His article on "Experience" for Baldwin's dictionary reflects just such an understanding of experience by defining it as:

> . . . the entire process of phenomena, of present data considered in their raw immediacy, before reflective thought has analyzed them into subjective and objective aspects or ingredients. It is the summum genus of which everything must have been a part before we can speak of it at all.115

In his _Pragmatism_, James takes a similar view of the primal and processive character of experience:

> All 'homes' are in finite experience; finite experience as such is homeless. Nothing outside of the flux secures the issue of it. It can hope salvation only from its own intrinsic promises and potencies.116

Still later, spelling out in his _Essays in Radical Empiricism_ what is entailed in the metaphysics of "pure experience," he says:

> Nothing shall be admitted as fact, it says, except what can be experienced at some definite time by some experient; and for every feature of fact ever so experienced, a definite place must be found somewhere in the final system of reality. In other words: Everything real must be experienceable, and every kind of thing experienced must somewhere be real.117

James's concept of "pure experience" is similar to his definition of "experience" in Baldwin. Pure experience is what is immediately there or given in experience, and it is "only virtually or potentially either object or subject."[118]   As he describes it in its phenomenological immediacy, there is again a suggestion of process:

> The instant field of the present is always experience in its 'pure' state, plain unqualified _actuality,_ a simple _that,_ as yet undifferentiated into thing and thought, and only virtually classifiable as objective fact or as someone's opinion about fact.[119]
> (First italics mine)

From these few glimpses into how James understands "experience" before and after the _Varieties,_ it is clear that he has an approach to experience broad enough to include religious experience and phenomeno- logical enough to see experience in its processive immediacy and primacy. In James's "experience" are the elements that Gendlin develops in his notion of "expe- riencing."

b) A Phenomenology of Feeling

Further perspective on James's understanding of the role of "feeling" in religion may be gained by seeing how "feeling" functions in other contexts. Since his use of "feeling" in his other writings is not overly consistent, it will be viewed here either as it parallels the _Varieties_ or as it seems to be a process.

In The Principles of Psychology James understands feeling within a "feeling-conceptual" contrast, but he also offers there a more direct or concrete phenomenol- ogy of individual feelings. He observes, for example, that feelings

> . . . are just exactly what we feel them, perfectly determinate conscious states, not vague editions of other conscious states. They may be faint and weak; they may be very vague cognizers of the same realities which other conscious states cognize and name exactly; they may be unconscious of much of the reality which other states are conscious

of. But that does not make them in them-selves a whit dim or vague or unconscious.[120]

Then, in a passage which anticipates Gendlin's "experiencing," James offers a concrete example of what he means by "feeling," an example which suggests that it is conscious, continuous, and unfolding, and yet is not identical with conceptualization:

> When I decide that I have, without knowing it, been for several weeks in love, I am sim-ply giving a name to a state which previously I have not named, but which was fully conscious; which had no residual mode of being except the manner in which it was con-scious; and which, though it was a feeling towards the same person for whom I now have a much more inflamed feeling, and though it continuously led into the latter, and is sim-ilar enough to be called by the same name, is yet in no sense identical with the latter, and least of all in any 'unconscious' way.[121]

James acknowledges how difficult it can be to dis-cover feelings and their relations by direct introspec-tion. Often there is no word to name the present feel-ing, and this "hinders the study of all but the very coarsest of them."[122] At times, the present feeling does not outlast the naming of it, but if it could, thinks James, the "state of feeling and the state of naming the feeling are continuous, and the infallibil-ity of such prompt introspective judgments is probably great."[123]

There are, in addition to this somewhat direct phenomenology of feeling evidenced in the Principles, four sets of contrasting concepts that parallel and give perspective to the general "feeling-conceptual" contrast of the Varieties. One perspective, which relates "feeling" with experience in its immediacy, is in the distinction James makes in the Principles between "knowledge of acquaintance" and "knowledge about." "Knowledge of acquaintance" stresses immediate experience as a starting point or as a prerequisite for knowledge; "knowledge about" is understood as a causal

28

explanation of why things are what they are. For example, I am acquainted with the color blue or the taste of a pear, but I cannot transmit knowledge about these things to someone who has not directly experienced them:

> I cannot _describe_ them, make a blind man guess what blue is like, define to a child a syllogism, or tell a philosopher in just what respect distance is just what it is, and differs from other forms of relation. At most, I can say to my friends, Go to certain places and act in certain ways, and these objects will probably come.[124]

A second perspective taken in the _Principles_ is a distinction between "feeling" and "thought." "Through feelings we become acquainted with things, but only by our thought do we know about them. Feelings are the germ and starting point, thoughts the developed tree."[125] The suggestion here is not only that feeling is primary, but that it is also part of a process ending in conceptualization. The process, however, is not one of simple maturation, but is rather a kind of reworking. Feeling is what is inwardly had in consciousness; in thought "we do more than merely have it; we seem as we think over its relations, to subject it to a sort of _treatment_ and to _operate_ upon it."[126]

A third perspective in the _Principles_ on the "feeling-conceptual" contrast lies in the distinction between the "transitive" and the "substantive" parts of the "stream of consciousness." From this perspective, while not neglecting the primal character of feeling, James's thinking clearly suggests that it is a flow or process.

> As we take, in fact, a general view of the wonderful stream of our consciousness, what strikes us first is this different pace of its parts. Like a bird's life, it seems to be made of an alternation of flights and perchings. The rhythm of language expresses this, where every thought is expressed in a sentence, and every sentence closed by a

period. The resting-places are usually occupied by sensorial imaginations of some sort, whose peculiarity is that they can be held before the mind for an indefinite time, and contemplated without changing; the places of flight are filled with thoughts of relations, static or dynamic, that for the most part obtain between matters contemplated in the periods of comparative rest.

Let us call the resting-places the "substantive parts," and the places of flight the "transitive parts," of the stream of thought. It then appears that the main end of our thinking is at all times the attainment of some other substantive part than the one from which we have just been dislodged. And we may say that the main use of the transitive parts is to lead us from one substantive conclusion to another.[127]

Trying to catch hold of the transitive parts is "like seizing a spinning top to catch its motion."[128] Still, James is unhappy with the failure to see the "feelings of relation," for example, supporting as an "unbroken stream" the substantive parts.[129]

Considering similar "feelings of tendency," which are feelings of what thoughts are going to arise next, he describes them as a supporting flow:

The traditional psychology talks like one who should say a river consists of nothing but pailsful, spoonsful, quartpotsful, barrelsful, and other moulded forms of water. Even were the pails and the pots all actually standing in the stream, still between them the free water would continue to flow. It is just this free water of consciousness that psychologists resolutely overlook. Every definite image in the mind is steeped and dyed in the free water that flows round it. With it goes the sense of its relations, near and remote, the dying echo of whence it came to us, the dawning sense of whither it is to lead.[130]

A fourth perspective on the "feeling-conceptual" contrast in the <u>Varieties</u> is the distinction James draws, especially in <u>Some</u> <u>Problems</u> <u>of</u> <u>Philosophy</u>, between "perception" and "conception." Here, again, perception is the "primordial" thing; it is immediate and real:

> The deeper features of reality are found only in perceptual experience. Here alone do we acquaint ourselves with continuity, or the immersion of one thing in another, here alone with self, with substance, with qualities, with activity in its various modes, with time, with cause, with change, with novelty, with tendency, with freedom.[131]

In this distinction, as in the one before, James mentions the element of change or process.

> Conceptual knowledge is forever inadequate to the fullness of the reality to be known. Reality consists of existential particulars as well as of essences and universals and class-names, and of existential particulars we become aware only in the perceptual flux. <u>The</u> <u>flux</u> <u>can</u> <u>never</u> <u>be</u> <u>superseded</u>, we must carry it with us to the bitter end of our cognitive business, keeping it in the midst of the translation even when the latter proves illuminating, and falling back on it alone when the translation gives out.[132] (Emphasis mine)

It is, in fact, the very inability of concepts to change that makes James so critical of the service they render:

> Conceptions form the one class of entities that cannot change under any circumstances. They can cease to be, altogether; or they can stay, as what they severally are; but there is for them no middle way. They form <u>an</u> <u>essentially</u> <u>discontinuous</u> system, and

translate the _process_ of our perceptual experience, which is _naturally a flux_, into a set of stagnant and petrified terms.[133] (Emphasis mine)

While most of James's observations on "conception" are in terms of its inadequacy and its misuse by philosophers, he does allow for a functional relationship between "perception" and "conception."

Perception awakens thought, and thought in turn enriches perception. The more we see, the more we think; while the more we think, the more we see in our immediate experiences, and the greater grows the detail, and the more significant the articulateness of our perception.[134]

In fact, in terms of an _ongoing process_, James see "perception" and "conception" as intimately interrelated.

Percepts and concepts interpenetrate and melt together, impregnate and fertilize each other. Neither, taken alone, knows reality in its completeness. We need them both, as we need both legs to walk with.[135]

4. Critical Reflections

Perhaps the most valuable contribution William James makes to the study of religion is simply the fact that he offers a phenomenology of religious experience. He takes both as data and starting point "what goes on in the single private man as he livingly expresses himself in religious faith and act."[136] His interest is in a science of religion which would "depend for its original material on facts of personal experience, and would have to square itself with personal experience through all its critical reconstructions."[137] In the _Varieties_ he is presenting the descriptions of Augustine and Tolstoy, Fox and Bunyan, along with his own, trying to use in an intelligible way the kinds of conceptualizations that emerge from the religious testimony itself. As Gordon Allport notes, whereas Sigmund

Freud seems to use reported instances of experience as exemplifications of a theory previously formed, there is in James's approach to religious experience much more of a tendency to let the categories suggest themselves out of the phenomena.[138] James is also quick to point out the difference in perspective between the outside observer and the one who has the experience. To the extent that he is an outside observer in religious matters, he respects the experience of others and tries to approach it on its own ground. As he remarks: "The only sound plan, if we are ourselves outside the pale of such emotions, is to observe as well as we are able those who feel them, and to record faithfully what we observe."[139] Clearly, James's approach to religion can be characterized as a phenomenology of personal religious experience.

The heart of this phenomenology of personal religious experience is religious feeling--his own and then that of others. In an analysis of the way James describes his own religious feeling, two characteristics are significant. First, in all of his descriptions, James is revealing what he _feels_ in relation to God. He is describing his own immediate sense of the divine. He is not just borrowing symbols from a religious tradition, nor is he offering an interpretation of the function or significance of God except as he directly experiences that function or significance in himself. Second, James finds within his experience a _sense_ of _reality_ of the divine. God is felt by him as real, however dimly or vaguely. The evolution of this sense of reality is from a vague feeling of security in a personal God to a more consciously needed, yet equally vague, sense of God as an ideal or as the aim and guarantee of personal striving.

James brings the same carefully objective description of what is there in his own religious feeling to his writing of the _Varieties_. Although he cannot be as directly phenomenological with the recorded experiences of others as he is with his own personal experience, still the role of feeling in these experiences easily surfaces. This feeling is defined as _primal_ and _foundational_. Religious concepts and systems are dependent on it for their meaning, while religious feeling itself is seen as an _irreducible_ and _non-rational_ phenomenon. There is _depth_ to religious feeling, and intimately connected with it is a sense of _facticity_ and _reality_, along with an immediate sense of _knowledge_ and _truth_.

Because James is so phenomenological in his observations of religious experience, he is able to focus on the object of religious feeling _as_ _that_ _object_ _is_ _revealed_ _within_ _feeling_. On the one hand, there _is_ a referent of religious feeling, for example, "God," "the divine," or "the higher power," and the feeling itself is the response to this referent. On the other hand, James does not say what this religious referent must be. It may be an objective entity, an ideal, or a wider consciousness, and the feeling response may be happiness, or fear, or striving, or security. The reason, in fact, why James can focus on religious feeling as actually felt is that he does not have a clearly articulated religious referent in mind. He does not start with a philosophical or creedal definition of the nature of God, and then look for an appropriate response in relation to it. Rather, his focus is on the _referent_ and _the_ _felt_ _response_ _as_ _they_ _are_ _revealed_ _together_ in the immediacy of experiencing. While he does talk about experiences which are of some religious object or referent, his concern is experiential or phenomenological rather than theological or denominational.

Although the thrust of James's thinking is very phenomenological, one criticism that can be offered, at least in terms of the _Varieties_, is that he is not phenomenological enough. His phenomenology slides back and forth, as it were, on a continuum that runs from an _immediate_ approach to religious feeling to an approach that can best be described as _distanced_. With his own religious feeling, as well as in some sections of the _Principles_, he focuses rather directly on feeling and lets the proper articulation come from it, but in the _Varieties_ he does not take this approach. In his "feeling-conceptual" contrast, what he says of feeling and its primacy seems often to be said not just because feeling is primary, but because conceptualization seems so inadequate. In other words, in the _Varieties_ there is often the sense that James is working from concepts

34

back to the primary feeling that must underlie them rather than starting with feeling and seeing how concepts flow from it. While he clearly adopts a phenomenology of religious experience in the Varieties, if that phenomenology were further specified, it would be as much a phenomenology of the inadequacy of religious concepts as a phenomenology of religious feeling.

One consequence of this distanced phenomenology of feeling is that in the Varieties, and even in much of the Principles, James has a difficult time spelling out an ongoing relationship between feeling and concepts. While he can say in the Varieties that feeling is "primary" and "living," this appears as a deduction from what is supposed to be "secondary" and "dependent" conceptualization. His approach in the Varieties is concept-to-feeling, and again, concept-to-feeling, with no way of ongoing living connection, no way to avoid a new exercise each time. Another consequence of his distanced phenomenology of feeling is that the feeling he wants to focus on is colored by the character of concepts, especially by the fact, which he often points out, that concepts are static and incapable of change. In a distanced phenomenology feeling appears static, already formed; its "living" quality becomes lost. In the Varieties, James puts religious feeling and the process of conversion or unification together, but he does not explain how they go together--even though in the earlier Principles, he offered a more immediate phenomenology of feeling which shows from several perspectives that feeling actually is a "flux" or "stream."

Some of this criticism of James's phenomenology of religious feeling is offered in light of the phenomenon of "religious experiencing" yet to be described. A case can be made, however, that an understanding of "living religion," that is, religion as some kind of feeling process which involves conversion and leads to saintliness, is a consistent concern for him. The thinking of Eugene Gendlin offers a very immediate and concrete phenomenology of feeling in the person. Gendlin describes feeling and process as one phenomenon which is meant to be a growth process, and at the same time, he offers a very insightful articulation of the relation between feeling and concepts. A careful exposition of Gendlin's thinking will help to answer some of the questions raised by James's phenomenology of feeling and will be extremely helpful in working toward an articulation of "religious experiencing."

ENDNOTES

1   See Friedrich Schleiermacher, On Religion: Speeches to its Cultured Despisers, Third German Edition, John Oman, trans., New York, Harper Torchbooks, 1958, and Friedrich Schleiermacher, The Christian Faith, Second German Edition, H. R. Mackintosh and J. S. Stewart, trans., Edinburgh, Clark, 1928. See also Rudolf Otto, The Idea of the Holy, John W. Harvey, trans., New York, Oxford University Press, 1958.

2   See James M. Edie, "William James and The Phenomenology of Religious Experience," American Philosophy and the Future: Essays for a New Generation, Michael Novak, ed., New York, Scribner's, 1968, p. 248. Edie states in the beginning of this article: "To some it may appear strange that James 'the pragmatist' should so forthrightly and without apologies be incorporated into the phenomenological viewpoint. But I want to show that James's methodological contributions to the study of religious experience are not only more sound phenomenologically than some of the studies which have, under the influence of Husserl, up to now explicitly invoked the phenomenological method, but that they are also the first to establish any solid basis for a true phenomenology of religious experience."
    Edward George Bozzo, "James and the Valence of Human Action," Journal of Religion and Health, Vol. 16, No. 1, January 1977, p. 27, observes: "In his phenomenological approach, James made an epoche of 'scientific' accounts of religious

experience, and an _epoche_ of doctrinal religious beliefs and theologies, in order to focus on invariant factors of human consciousness, especially those that manifest themselves with special clarity in religious experience."

An insightful explication of James's phenomenology of religious experience is found in Ronald M. Gilmore, "William James and Religious Language: Daughters of Earth, Sons of Heaven?" _Eglise et Theologie_, Vol. 4, No. 3, 1973, p. 359-390.

For an excellent perspective on phenomenology in James's psychology as a whole see Hans Linschoten, _On the Way Toward a Phenomenological Psychology: The Psychology of William James_, Pittsburgh, Duquesne University Press, 1968, and Bruce Wilshire, _William James and Phenomenology: A Study of "The Principles of Psychology,"_ Bloomington, Indiana University Press, 1968. See also Ash Gobar, "The Phenomenology of William James," _Proceedings of The American Philosophical Society_, Vol. 114, No. 4, August 1970, p. 294-309.

A clear exposition of James's understanding of "affectivity" and "feeling" from a phenomenological perspective is offered by James F. Brown, _Affectivity: Its Language and Meaning_, Washington, University Press of America, 1982.

3   _The Varieties of Religious Experience_ is the published version of the Gifford Lectures on Natural Religion given by James at Edinburgh University during the 1901-1902 academic year.

4   Ralph Barton Perry, _The Thought and Character of William James_, Vol. I, Boston, Little, Brown, 1935, p. 130.

5   William James, "Introduction," _The Literary Remains of the Late Henry James_, William James, ed., Boston, Osgood, 1885, p. 15-16.

6   Perry, _The Thought and Character of William James_, Vol. I, p. 467.

7   Maurice Le Breton, _The Religion of William James_, Cambridge, Harvard University Press, 1926, p. 5.

8 William James, <u>The Varieties of Religious Experience</u>, Cambridge, Harvard University Press, 1985, p. 134.

9 <u>Ibid</u>., p. 135.

10 <u>Ibid</u>.

11 William James, "Diary 1868," MS Box L, James Archives, Houghton Library, Harvard University, Cambridge.

12 Ralph Barton Perry, <u>The Thought and Character of William James</u>, Vol. II, Boston, Little, Brown, 1935, p. 353.

13 <u>Ibid</u>., Vol. I, p. 737.

14 William James, "Another non-religious type," in "J. Memoranda for Gifford Lectures. Original Plan for a philosophical second volume. 1900 plus," Notebooks, MS Box L, James Archives, Houghton Library, Harvard University, Cambridge. From the way James reworks this manuscript it is clear that he is talking about himself.

15 <u>The Letters of William James</u>, Vol. II, Henry James, ed., Boston, Atlantic Monthly Press, 1920, p. 211.

16 James, <u>The Varieties of Religious Experience</u>, p. 301.

17 <u>Ibid</u>., p. 308.

18 William James, "A Suggestion About Mysticism," <u>Collected Essays and Reviews</u>, Ralph Barton Perry, ed., New York, Russell & Russell, 1969, p. 501. James tells here of four quasi-mystical experiences which occurred shortly before he died in 1910.

19 One of James's earlier reviews is a sympathetic reception of <u>Anaesthetic Revelation</u> by the mystic Benjamin Paul Blood; see <u>Atlantic Monthly</u>,

Vol. 34, 1874, p. 627-629.

20 William James, "On Some Hegelisms," _Mind_, Vol. 7, No. 26, April 1882, note, p. 206. It is interesting to mention in passing that Charles Tart says of James's description of the effects of nitrous oxide: "I do not know of any better account of the phenomenology of the nitrous oxide experience." See Charles T. Tart, _Altered States of Consciousness_, New York, Doubleday, 1972, p. 330.

21 Gerald Heard, "Can This Drug Enlarge Man's Mind?" _The Psychedelic Reader_, Gunther M. Weil, Ralph Metzner, and Timothy Leary, eds., New York, Citadel, 1971, p. 9.

22 _The Letters of William James_, Vol. II, p. 76-77.

23 George Santayana, _Character and Opinion in the United States_, New York, Norton, 1967, p. 82.

24 John Elof Boodin, "William James as I Knew Him, II," _The Personalist_, Vol. 23, No. 2, Summer 1942, p. 285.

25 Ralph Barton Perry, _The Thought and Character of William James_ (Briefer Version), New York, Harper Torchbooks, 1964, p. 253.

26 William James, "Theology School Lectures," "Religion After 1897," MS Box H, James Archives, Houghton Library, Harvard University, Cambridge.

27 _The Letters of William James_, Vol. II, p. 127. David Hay, "Re-Review: William James' _The Varieties of Religious Experience_," _The Modern Churchman_, N.S., XXVII, No. 2, 1985, p. 49, confirms what James is concerned about in his approach to religion: "He is too honest and too sensitive a man to accept secular dismissals of his religion, or on the other hand to find an easy resting place for it in our cultural tradition as it stands."

28 Fredson Bowers, prep., "The Text of _The Varieties_

of Religious Experience," The Varieties of Religious Experience. p. 573.

29 Perry, The Thought and Character of William James, Vol. I, p. 165-166.

30 Perry, The Thought and Character of William James (Briefer Version), p. 259.

31 James, The Varieties of Religious Experience, p. 341.

32 Ibid.

33 Ibid., p. 66-67.

34 Ibid., p. 67.

35 Ibid.

36 Ibid.

37 Ibid., p. 342.

38 Ibid.

39 Ibid., p. 340.

40 Ibid., p. 342.

41 Ibid., p. 341.

42 Ibid., p. 397. James's "feeling" and "feelings" reflect more than single and plural usage. "Feeling" often seems to connote for him a deeper, non-rational, living reality of the individual. "Feelings" often seem to be surface manifestations and concept-like emotional contents of "feeling."

43 Ibid., p. 68.

44 Ibid., p. 67.

45 Ibid.

46 Ibid., p. 341.

47 Ibid., p. 156.

48 Ibid., p. 359.

49 Ibid., p. 358-359.

50 Ibid., p. 393.

51 Ibid., p. 393-394.

52 Ibid., p. 394.

53 Ibid.

54 Ibid., p. 395.

55 Ibid., p. 66.

56 Ibid.

57 Ibid., p. 67.

58 Ibid., p. 359.

59 Ibid., p. 360.

60 Ibid., p. 67.

61 Ibid., p. 96.

62 Ibid., p. 302. It should be noted that the "feeling-conceptual" contrast is not always understood
by James in the same way. Originally the Varieties was to be in two parts, the first, descrip-
tive, and the second, philosophical. In what
remains of this philosophical part James's pragmatism comes into play as an inquiry into the
question of the truth of what is revealed in religious feeling. In his "Conclusions," p. 401, for
example, James introduces a distinction between
religious feelings as "only psychological phenomena" and the question of "the objective 'truth'
of their content." In this instance, and in oth-

ers as well, James shifts his approach from phenomenological or experiential to empirical. Truth is no longer from within the experience, but it comes from some other (pragmatic) criteria, and there is a concomitant shift from the primacy of feeling over conceptualization to a primacy of conceptualization and interpretation over concrete feeling.

63 Ibid., p. 34.

64 Ibid., p. 36.

65 Ibid., p. 39.

66 Ibid., p. 55. This passage shows that James, in contrast to Freud, is willing to allow the categories of psychology to be challenged by a phenomenology of the unique way divine reality actually seems to be experienced. In light of James's phenomenological approach, it is surprising to find Rudolf Otto, The Idea of the Holy, p. 11, note 1, pointing to this passage in criticizing James's "empiricist and pragmatist standpoint."

67 Ibid., p. 39.

68 Ibid., p. 39-40.

69 Ibid., p. 59.

70 Ibid., p. 53.

71 Ibid., p. 294.

72 Ibid., p. 31.

73 Ibid.

74 Ibid., p. 78.

75 Ibid., p. 72.

76 Ibid., p. 71.

77 Ibid.

78 Ibid., p. 72.

79 Ibid., p. 198.

80 Ibid., p. 201.

81 Ibid., p. 202.

82 Ibid., "Saintliness," p. 210-261.

83 Ibid., p. 330.

84 Ibid., p. 219-220.

85 Ibid., p. 146 and 147.

86 Ibid., p. 123.

87 Ibid., p. 124.

88 Ibid., p. 132.

89 Ibid., p. 142.

90 Ibid., p. 135.

91 Ibid., p. 122.

92 Ibid., p. 131.

93 Ibid.

94 Ibid., p. 146.

95 Ibid.

96 Ibid., p. 95.

97 Ibid.

98 Ibid., p. 169.

99 Ibid., p. 162.

100 <u>Ibid</u>.

101 <u>Ibid</u>.

102 <u>Ibid</u>.

103 <u>Ibid</u>., p. 163.

104 <u>Ibid</u>.

105 <u>Ibid</u>.

106 <u>Ibid</u>.

107 <u>Ibid</u>., p. 164.

108 <u>Ibid</u>., p. 171.

109 <u>Ibid</u>., p. 172.

110 <u>Ibid</u>.

111 <u>Ibid</u>., p. 173.

112 <u>Ibid</u>.

113 See Richard Stevens, <u>James and Husserl</u>: <u>The</u> <u>Foundations</u> of <u>Meaning</u>, The Hague, Martinus Nijhoff, 1974, p. 6. See also A. J. Ayer, <u>The</u> <u>Origins</u> of <u>Pragmatism</u>, London, Macmillan, 1968, p. 190.

114 William James, <u>A Pluralistic Universe</u>, Cambridge, Harvard University Press, 1977, p. 135.

115 William James, "'Experience,': from Baldwin's <u>Dictionary</u>," <u>Essays in Philosophy</u>, Cambridge, Harvard University Press, 1978, p. 95.

116 William James, <u>Pragmatism</u>, Cambridge, Harvard University Press, 1978, p. 125.

117 William James, <u>Essays in Radical Empiricism</u>, Cambridge, Harvard University Press, 1976, p. 81.

118 <u>Ibid</u>., p. 13.

119 <u>Ibid</u>., p. 36-37.

120 William James, <u>The</u> <u>Principles</u> <u>of</u> <u>Psychology</u>, Vol. I, Cambridge, Harvard University Press, 1981, p. 175.

121 <u>Ibid</u>.

122 <u>Ibid</u>., p. 194.

123 <u>Ibid</u>., p. 190, note 8.

124 <u>Ibid</u>., p. 217.

125 <u>Ibid</u>., p. 218.

126 <u>Ibid</u>.

127 <u>Ibid</u>., p. 236. It should be noted that James's uses of the word "thought" is problematic. What he is looking for in the <u>Principles</u> is a word that covers "every form of consciousness indiscriminately" (p. 219-220). At times he uses "thought" to define what he finds in experience, and at other times he uses "feeling." He seems more comfortable with a use of "feeling" as characterizing immediate experience, and since he opposes "feeling" and "thought" (as in the second perspective mentioned above), very often the sense of what he is saying is only captured by understanding "feeling" when the word "thought" is used. It is more accurate, for example, to understand "The Stream of Feeling" for the chapter in the <u>Principles</u> entitled "The Stream of Thought."

128 <u>Ibid</u>., p. 237.

129 <u>Ibid</u>., p. 239-240.

130 <u>Ibid</u>., p. 246.

131 William James, <u>Some</u> <u>Problems</u> <u>of</u> <u>Philosophy</u>, Cambridge, Harvard University Press, 1979, p. 54.

132 Ibid., p. 45.

133 James, The Principles of Psychology, p. 442.

134 James, Some Problems of Philosophy, p. 59.

135 Ibid., p. 34.

136 Perry, The Thought and Character of William James (Briefer Version), p. 259.

137 James, The Varieties of Religious Experience, p. 360.

138 Gordon Allport, The Use of Personal Documents in Psychological Science, New York, Social Science Research Council, 1942, p. 7 and 10.

139 James, The Varieties of Religious Experience, p. 261.

CHAPTER TWO

EUGENE GENDLIN:

THE EXPERIENCING PROCESS

By looking at the major elements of Eugene Gendlin's notion of "experiencing," this chapter furthers James's description of "feeling" as a process. "Experiencing"--the concept and the phenomenon--has a clear contribution to make to an understanding of religion as a personal, living process. On the one hand, it is a conceptual link between James's findings at the turn of the Century concerning the nature of religious feeling and the contemporary organismic view of therapeutic change and growth. On the other hand, it allows for an understanding of "religious experiencing" as an actually felt religious phenomenon which can be described and evoked.

One way Gendlin describes "experiencing" is by showing how it arises as a way of understanding what takes place in the process of therapy:

> When therapists discuss cases, they use rough metaphoric terms to refer to a feeling process. They often say that they observe clients "emotionally absorbing something," or "working through," or "feeling through." The therapeutic process is observed to include not only concepts, but also a feeling process . . .[1]

Gendlin calls this feeling process "experiencing." It is not just _there_ with the concepts, but, as James also found, this feeling process seems to underlie

47

them. If, for example, you were to ask yourself how
you were feeling right now, you would have to stop and
pay attention to your present "experiencing" to see
what is there. Then you would search for the right
words to say what that is. You might say: "I'm a bit
tired right now." These words might not seem just
right, so maybe you would say: "It's more like I'm a
little distracted . . . there's a discomfort . . .
almost a sense of uneasiness." This might say pretty
much what your present feeling is like, and you might
experience a slight shift in yourself, as if your body
were agreeing with your words. Then, if you continue
to stay with your present feeling, you might find yourself saying with a sense of really having found what is
there: "Ah! What I'm really feeling is I don't want to
tackle this second chapter before dinner." The words
you use come directly from the present feeling, and
only the right words will do. The words are helpful
because they point to, explicate, and further your process of "experiencing."

This presently felt, directly-referred-to "experiencing" or "feeling," and the way that meaningful
words or symbols come from it, is the subject of Gendlin's research. In this chapter, "experiencing" is
viewed from several perspectives, each with clear
implications for the "religious experiencing" described
in the next chapter.

1. A Basic Description of Experiencing

a) Experiencing, Existence, and Living

Much of Gendlin's thinking comes out of a creative
interaction with existential philosophy and phenomenology. His theory of "experiencing" is really a theory
of existence as lived. From an existential perspective, experiencing is our concrete sense of being
alive. It is what each of us as a concrete individual
feels, lives, and experiences. "Existence," says Gendlin, "is always yours, mine, his. It is the concrete
ongoing living we feel and are."[2] He observes, in fact
that "it is doubtful that there is such a thing as
'you' apart from the flow of experiencing, which most
truly is what you every moment are."[3]

This experiencing or living process is organismic. It is the bodily "feel" that each of us has of his or her own existence. "The sense of, and access to existence is the life of the body as felt from inside, 'your sense of being your living body just now.'"4

What is meant by the experiencing process? It is felt. It is the most obvious thing in the world. It is our sense of being alive, our bodily sense, our feeling process. The experiencing process is your being here, now. It is you. You are looking out through your eyes from it. You are a feeling process. You are not words or thoughts. I am not letting you think your own words. If you are following me you have my words. My words are echoing in your head. But that does not make you be me. You are still here. You are not these words. You are a concrete experiential feeling process.5 (Emphasis mine)

For the most part, "experiencing" and "feeling" are interchangeable, provided feeling is understood not as a noun but as a verb, as the feeling activity.6 Gendlin insists that "feeling is a concrete living process, a living-in-situations, not a container of picturable contents."7 This concrete living or experiencing is always there as "how" or "what" we feel. At any time, we can directly refer to or attend to this present feeling. Gendlin uses the word "feeling" precisely because it refers to concrete existence in its livingness.

b) Experiencing as Situated and Interacting

Although, on occasion, Gendlin employs the modifier "subjective" to help locate experiencing, his understanding of experiencing or feeling is no more subjective than that of James. As Gendlin explains:

What one feels at any given moment is always interactional, it is a living in an infinite universe and in situations, a context of other people, of words, and signs, of physical surroundings, of events past, present and future. Experiencing is not "subjective," but interactional, not intra-psychic, but interactional. It is not inside but inside-outside.[8]

In other words, experiencing is concretely felt _inwardly_ and situationally felt _outwardly_. A context of organism-environment is implicit in it.

A person is a _bodily_ interaction with others and with his environment, much as breathing is a bodily interaction with an environment. How one lives and reacts is a bodily process going on in situations. When someone is about to jump at you, you feel it in your "gut." When someone is in complicated ways going to hurt you, again you feel it in your gut. Just as a golfer feels in his body, in the position of his feet, and in the muscular sense of his swing, the whole scene in front of him, so do we bodily experience the complexity of our situations and interactions.[9]

"Feeling is how we are alive in the environment, and therefore we feel, in a bodily way, the whole context of our living."[10] Take anger, for example:

We always feel angry at what someone did because of what happened to us and what we must now do. We never feel anger at just something subjective, an entity within, unrelated to the world we live in. What we actually experience eliminates the old barrier between the objective (geometrically conceived atoms and physical forces outside) and the subjective (entities or forces inside).[11]

In his understanding of "experiencing" or "feeling," Gendlin avoids any subject-object split. Feeling cannot be defined apart from environment; experiencing _is_ situated interacting. "There is no internal/external split; we feel internally our living in the external situation."[12] While language tends to dichotomize experience, feeling, when focused on directly, does not.

It is an error to think of situations as already cut up neatly and tritely, so that they need only be observed and stated, just as it is an error to think of feelings as featureless masses unrelated to situations or words. We have feelings in and of situations. Conversely, situations are not physical facts but predicaments for people's living, desiring and avoiding. Situation and experience cannot be separated . . .[13]

c) Experiencing as Preconceptual and as Guiding Conceptualization

Having described "experiencing" as living and situated, Gendlin points to the fact that this process is also preconceptual and endlessly differentiable. In a way redolent of James, he observes:

One exists one's concrete experiencing and this is not equal to concepts, conceptual patterns, definitions, or units of any kind. Patterns and units can be made from experiencing, but experiencing is never equal to what words we say, or to any "what," which one might define.[14]

Gendlin explains further what he means, when he says:

If experiencing were conceptual, or even logically determined, then if divided in some way, all further ways it could be divided would have to be consistent with the first way. Only those further aspects could occur which would logically fit with the first. In fact, experiencing is preconceptual and can be differentiated into very many sub-aspects, all then directly felt, more than any conceptual scheme can handle.[15]

Much like James before him, Gendlin is positing a primacy of "experiencing" or "feeling" over conceptu-

51

alization. "The experiences are not defined by the concepts, but, on the contrary, the concepts are defined by the steps of experiencing."[16] Often this primal experiencing is vague in the sense that it cannot easily be named or differentiated conceptually, yet it may not be at all vague in the sense of its "being there." Speaking of a present feeling, he says,

> It may be vague only in that we may not know what it is. We can put only a few aspects of it into words. The mass itself is always something there, no matter what we say "it is." Our definitions, our knowing "what it is," are symbols that specify aspects of it, "parts' of it, as we say. Whether we name it, divide it, or not, there it is.[17]

For Gendlin, not only is there a primacy of feeling, but, as in the thinking of James, there also is a cognitive element in feeling which he calls "implicit meaning." "Experiencing" or "feeling" is implicitly meaningful. In other words, there is meaning in experiencing, although this meaning may be only implicitly felt and not yet, perhaps, differentiated explicitly with words or symbols:

> Here is something we call a "feeling," something felt in a physical sense, yet later on the individual will say that certain concepts now accurately represent that feeling. The feeling, he will say, was such and so all along, but he didn't know it. He only felt it. He felt it in such a unique and specific way the he could gradually, by directly referring to it, arrive at concepts for it. That is to say, the feeling was implicitly meaningful. It had a meaning which was distinguishably different from other feelings and meanings, but its meaning was felt rather than known in explicit symbols.[18]

"Experiencing" or "feeling" is of meanings which are preconceptual in themselves, but which must be looked to as the basis of conceptualization.

Experiencing guides conceptualization; it is in a sense primary in that some explicit meanings may "fit" it and some may not. To find the right meaning the person may often have to refer back to his present experiencing to see what its explicit meaning is. Often there are many more meanings in present, concrete experiencing than could be made explicit, and also this present ongoing experiencing could be conceptualized in many different ways.[19]

Like James, Gendlin sees truth in feeling in the sense that when the right words come, we know if they are true. We can _feel_ the truth, even though the words themselves are a "running truth" and may need to change as experiencing is ongoing.[20]

d) Experiencing as Explicated Conceptually and Symbolically

Experiencing is preconceptual, yet it guides conceptualization. The tendency, therefore, is to see feeling as essentially the same as concepts, only nonconceptual. But Gendlin insists that experiencing is not made up of hidden conceptual units:

I must now make it quite clear that "implicit" and "explicit" meanings are different in nature. We may feel that some verbal statement says exactly what we mean; nevertheless, to feel the meaning is not the same kind of thing as verbal symbols. As we have shown, a felt meaning can contain very many meanings and can be further and further elaborated. Thus the felt meaning is not the same in kind as the precise symbolized explicit meaning. The reason the difference in kind is so important is because if we ignore it we assume that explicit meanings are (or were) already in the implicit felt meaning. We are led to make the felt, implicit meaning a kind of dark place in which countless explicit meanings are hidden. We then wrongly assume that these meanings are "implicit" and felt only in that they are "hidden." I must emphasize that the "implicit" or "felt" datum of experiencing is a sensing of body life. As such it may have countless organized aspects, but this does not mean that they are conceptually formed, explicit, and hidden. Rather, we complete and form them when we explicate.[21]

While experiencing is different "in kind" from conceptualization, it needs symbols to point to it and to form it. It needs a word, or image, or action, or event, or interpersonal response, in short, anything which can refer to present experiencing to capture and complete it. And this capturing or completing is itself felt. When words or symbols of some kind "fit" present experiencing, there is an experiential effect. A felt shift or release is experienced.[22]

When we differentiate and symbolize a felt meaning by using words (just those words which, at the moment, feel exactly right), a physical felt change or 'referent movement' occurs, indicating that one alters the felt meaning by accurately symbolizing it.[23]

One of the most significant of Gendlin's findings is not only that there is an interdependence between feeling and conceptualization, but that when feeling is paid direct attention to, their relationship is a process of ongoing interaction and change. In other words, experiencing as an ongoing process is an interacting with words or symbols--specifically with those words or symbols which can capture and complete it, and in so doing change it and carry the process of experiencing further.

When an individual expresses accurately for the first time how he is, just then and in precisely in so doing he is no longer that way. The accuracy which he feels so deeply-- the physically sensed release of the words which feel exactly right--this very feeling is the feeling of change, or resolution, of experiencing moving a step forward.[24]

In discussing the relation between "experiencing"
and "concepts," the nature of experiencing as a therapeutic process begins to surface. One way to introduce
a consideration of therapeutic change is to look more
closely at "concepts" and how they function.

Experiential Concepts

In Gendlin's understanding, every concept has a
logical and a felt aspect, although even the logical
aspect must at some time have been in relation to
experiencing.

> What really is a concept? A concept is
> both logical and felt. It is a logical con-
> struct but since it is also a thought, it has
> a "soft underbelly," it is made of felt sens-
> ing. We "know what it means" or "what we
> mean by using it" . . . we know what we mean
> with it in a felt sensing way. We mean with
> the concept to make a certain point, to take
> exception to an aspect of what has been said,
> to point out certain things which are impor-
> tant because . . . and so on . . .[25]

Gendlin stresses the rootedness of the concept in
the felt sensing or felt meaning of experiencing:

> We cannot even know what a concept "means"
> or use it meaningfully without the "feel" of
> its meaning. No amount of symbols, defini-
> tions, and the like can be used in the place
> of felt meaning. If we do not have the felt
> meaning of the concept, we haven't got the
> concept at all--only a verbal noise.[26]

For a concept, as Gendlin defines it, two things
are necessary: experiencing or felt meaning and the
verbal symbol. In fact, the real definition of the
concept from an experiential perspective is that it is
the relation between the two.

> Concepts are relationships between felt
> meanings and linguistic symbols. The lin-
> guistic symbols are really only noises or

sound images of noises--except in so far as they relate to felt meanings. Only as we have the felt meaning, do we have the meaning of the concept. Only with the felt meanings of concepts do we think. It is thus the very nature of concepts that they consist not only of noises but also of felt meanings.[27]

One finding of Gendlin's research on the therapeutic process is that the logical use of concepts does not bring about change. "One can, and often does, move directly from concept to concept by conceptual implication. But therapeutic change and resolution occur because of those times one moves via intervening experiential steps."[28] Only an experiential use of concepts, only words or symbols which directly refer to or interact with concrete experiencing have a therapeutic effect. As Gendlin says: "All psychotherapists and psychotherapy patients know the difference between statements that are merely true and --much rarer-- statements which make an experiential difference."[29]

Although, in the context of therapy, concepts may be used by the therapist which have explanatory meaning, often these concepts do not touch the client's actual experiencing.

> The concepts do not tell us the underlying dynamics. Concretely felt experiential meanings really "underlie." Concepts have real meaning only as they are made to refer to some of these specific and firmly differentiated aspects of felt meanings. In so using concepts, the meaning resides in the felt meanings one concretely refers to. The concept is a pointer. Concepts have only a poor, nearly empty general meaning, when not used in direct reference to aspects of felt meanings. The aspects of felt meaning one finds are so very much more specific, and shift in such nonlogical modes, that aside from this use in pointing and differentiating, the concepts are not at all explanatory of anyone.[30]

The function of an experiential use of concepts in therapy is that they directly interact with experiencing in a way that captures, completes, and furthers that experiencing. In a broader philosophical context, Gendlin discusses other ways in which concepts or symbols interact with experiencing. What he insists on, however, is that the words we use and the statements we make must always be in interplay with present experiencing, if there is to be an experiential effect and the experiencing process is to be carried forward.[31]

Although the integration of Gendlin's thinking with that of James is part of the next chapter, already it is evident that Gendlin's phenomenology of "experiencing" furthers the contribution that James's phenomenology makes to the rehabilitation of "feeling." Gendlin's work reveals:

a) that feeling can be referred to <u>directly</u> and need not be seen through a distanced phenomenology;

b) that the <u>primacy</u> of feeling comes from the fact that it <u>is</u> the living felt process of the person;

c) that feeling is a preconceptual matrix different <u>in kind</u> from concepts and not just something similar but non-verbal;

d) that feeling, when directly referred to, is a <u>continuous</u>, implicitly meaningful process which concepts or symbols can endlessly differentiate. In other words, there is a continuing flow of feeling-to-concept, not a series of static analytic exercises of concept-to-feeling and, again, concept-to-feeling;

e) that feeling, while primary and foundational, is also an interacting with concepts or symbols which carries the experiencing process forward.

2. <u>Therapeutic</u> and <u>Interpersonal</u>
<u>Aspects</u> of <u>Experiencing</u>

In "A Theory of Personality Change," an article which relates "experiencing" to psychotherapy, Gendlin mentions two observations about personality change that he feels most theorists accept:

(1) Major personality change involves some sort of intense affective or feeling process occurring in the individual.

(2) Major personality change occurs nearly always in the context of an ongoing personal relationship.[32]

This first observation, about an "intense affective or feeling process," is the concern of the opening part of this section. It begins with the procedure of "focusing," taught as a step-by-step way of paying attention to "experiencing." Then, it describes the process of change as this process unfolds, ideally, in four phases. The second observation, about "an ongoing personal relationship," is the concern of the final part of this section. It looks at the role of an interpersonal relationship and at its significance for the quality of the experiencing process.

a) "Focusing" and Therapeutic Change

Gendlin has developed an experiential procedure called "focusing," which is a therapeutic way of helping a person pay attention to present experiencing so that it can change, shift, and open up in an ongoing way. The ability to "focus" is a skill which is usually not hard to learn but which is a way of self-relating not ordinarily engaged in.

Usually a person tells himself or herself how he or she is feeling, what is wrong, what the problem is. "Focusing" is a complete shift in direction. If the person can stop and pay attention to present experiencing, gradually _it_ will say what it is. The process of "focusing" is not only a step-by-step coming to know what is there, but, concomitantly, it is also an organismic way of being released, changed, and carried further in the situation. In "focusing" words come from experiencing, and _these_ words reflect a felt difference in the way one is living.

Just how does a person actually do "focusing"? In recent years, Gendlin has been developing ways of teaching the process in six steps. These six steps are presented here in an appropriation of some of his various descriptions.[33]

The Six Steps of Focusing

1. Clearing a Space

This first step is very important for the beginning of focusing. Even if you are aware of the problem or situation you want to focus on, it helps to clear some space for it by taking an inventory of the other things the organism is presently concerned about. Usually the problem you are aware of will surface along with the others.

You prepare for this step by finding a place, alone or with the one helping you, where you will not be disturbed. Then you let yourself get physically comfortable (it is best not to lie down). You might stretch and take a few deep breaths to relax and be aware of your body.

Now, let your attention be inside, in your chest or stomach area in the middle of your body, and see how you feel there and what comes when you ask yourself: "How am I now? How am I feeling right now? What's the main thing for me right now?" Wait, and see what comes. You are looking for your body, the organism, to tell you what it is living right now. Sometimes it helps to say to yourself: "Everything's fine right now, isn't it?" Again, wait, and see what comes.

Whatever comes, welcome it in a friendly way, but don't go into it. Just place it down "outside" you, so you can get a little space from it, knowing that you can come back to it if you want to. Then, again, put your attention inside, wait, and see what else comes, what other problems or situations your organism is presently living. As the felt sense of each new problem or situation comes, welcome it, and again, place it down outside yourself. If you find it hard to put the felt sense of a situation outside yourself, then say to yourself: "How would I feel if I didn't have this thing, or if it were all resolved?" The sense of relief that comes bodily is what you are after; that's the space.

Take a few moments to clear a space for yourself.

59

Typically, there may be four or five things that come, some major and some less significant, some you were pretty much aware of and some, perhaps, you were not aware of at all. At the end of the process you should feel some distance, some freedom, some breathing space between "yourself" and "all those things" you welcomed and put outside yourself. You should be able to say: "Well, except for all those things, everything feels just fine with me."

2. The Felt Sense

This second step is the heart of focusing, because in this step you begin to pay direct attention to your present experiencing of some given problem or situation.

See which of the things that came as you cleared a space now feels most important to focus on. The organism knows what it is carrying, so often the most important thing to pay attention to seems to suggest itself. If it doesn't, choose the one you want to pay attention to now. If you are new to this process, a simple concern might be best to choose. Whatever it is, try not to let it rush back inside. Keep the space between "it" and "you."

Now see if you can't get a felt sense, in the middle of your body, of what it feels like to have this situation or concern. Pay attention to where you usually feel things, and see if you can't sense what the whole thing feels like. If you find it difficult to get the sense of the way the whole of it is for you, it may be helpful to say to yourself: "This thing (problem or situation you are focusing on) is all O.K., isn't it? It feels just fine to have it, doesn't it?" Wait, and usually the felt sense of the problem will form.

Three things are important in this step, and, in fact, in all the steps. First, you need to be friendly or empathic with yourself in the focusing. An angry, self-critical attitude clamps the process and keeps it from unfolding. Second, you need to be patient and allow the felt sense to come; usually it is not just there. Third, since analyzing is such a natural tendency for almost everyone, you may need to make a conscious effort not to do that. Say to yourself: "No, for now let me stay with the _felt_ version of the problem."

Almost always, at first, the felt sense is quite vague and unfocused. As you give yourself a minute just to stay with it, usually it becomes clearer, stronger, more distinctly formed and felt. If the felt sense of a problem should come rushing back too strongly and you find yourself overwhelmed, sometimes it helps to imagine there is a door between you and the felt situation. You can open the door just a crack to let in the smallest bit of the feeling, just enough to get a sense of it. If you are still overwhelmed, or if you find yourself too anxious to proceed, or if you find yourself getting lost in bad feeling, you should stop. Being overwhelmed and lost in a bad feeling are not helpful, and they are not focusing. Someone competent to help you with focusing or a good psychotherapist may be needed.

3. The Handle

The third step is the beginning of the conceptualization or symbolization of experiencing in order to capture, complete, and carry it forward as an ongoing process.

As you let yourself stay with the felt sense of the whole of the problem or situation, see if, _without analyzing_, a "handle," that is, a word, a phrase, or an image, won't come to say exactly what the felt sense is like. Often a "quality word" will come first to capture the sense of the whole thing, a word like "heavy," "stuck," "helpless," or "scary." Or there may be a phrase like "all tied up" or "it's hard to breathe." Or there may be an image such as "it's a tight ball." Stay with the felt sense of the problem until words or an image come to fit it just right.

When the words or image fit just right, often there is a bodily felt shift, a kind of opening up, and already in the next moment the experiencing is different. This shift and opening up is the kind of thing you are looking for, but you can't make it happen except by letting just the right word or image come from the felt sense of the situation. When this happens, more words may then come to describe more of the felt sense.

4. Resonating

This step is a way to check and see if the "handle" you found in the previous step is really the right one to hold the whole of the "felt sense."

In this step you go back and forth between the felt sense and the handle. You must let yourself stay with the felt sense of the problem (this is always the bottom line in focusing) and let the words or image change, if they need to, to fit exactly. So you might say, for example, "Heavy? Is that how it feels?" And then you wait to see if there isn't at least a slight body movement of recognition, an ease in breathing or maybe a slight shifting of the shoulders. "Heavy" may not be quite right, and as you stay with the felt sense you have inside, a phrase like "it's just too much" may come, and this may be what fits exactly. Resonate again to be sure.

With the resonating, or even before when the word or image came, or even before that, the felt sense may have already changed, simply because you have paid attention to it. Let the felt sense change in any way that it wants to. Welcome and stay with whatever comes. Again, wait and let the right words or image come from the new felt sense that you have. Your experiencing process is unfolding step by step, and you can be with it until it feels either resolved or all right to stop.

5. Asking

The purpose of this fifth step in focusing is to help bring about a shift or change in the felt sense, if that still needs to occur. This change is not just something subjective, not just something that "feels good" inside. "Experiencing" is the way you are living in your environment, in your situations. The change that comes from focusing is a fresh, less constricted, and more alive way of being in a situation. Although it may take a number of rounds to get there, this is the kind of change you are after.

Often what comes through "resonating" the "handle" with the "felt sense" is a definite but slight body shift of recognition, for example, "Heavy, yes that's how it feels." What you want to occur is a shift in the way you are living in the situation. If you can be patient and let yourself stay with the felt sense of the situation and resonate the handle, often the shift will come. One way to help the shift to come is to ask the felt sense directly something about itself.

As you stay with the felt sense and resonate it so that it is not just remembered but bodily felt in the present, see if it helps to ask into it: "What about this situation makes it so _____? (here you use the handle, for example, "heavy" or "hard to breathe"). Wait, and see what comes. When you ask a question into the felt sense it is easy to get a quick answer that you have already figured out or know. If you get an answer like that, let it go. Wait, and see if something won't come _from the feeling_, that is, words along with a shift in the felt sense. If, after a moment, this question does not seem to help, you can try another question (still staying with the felt sense of the problem and the handle). Ask into it: "What's the worst of all of this?" Again, wait, and see if this question helps. Or you might ask into the felt sense a question like "What needs to happen here." These questions are ways of touching the felt sense to help it move and open up.

6. Receiving

Gendlin also calls this step "making a good space for what has come."[34] Although, as an attitude, it is helpful at every step along the way, this "receiving" is especially helpful when a felt sense has shifted and opened up. Stay for a while with what has come. Welcome it, savor it, take time to be with it. If you are going to do another round of focusing, rest a moment first.

The essence of these six steps is simply staying with present experiencing (the felt sense of a situation) and letting words or symbols come from it which bring a bodily shift in the experiencing. Focusing, however, is a skill, which for most people is easiest to learn with the help of another person who knows the process. The helping person can tailor the instructions to you and can give you whatever feedback you need not to get lost.[35]

The instructions for the six steps have a generous sprinkling of words like "usually," "often," and "maybe." Each person tends to focus in his or her own unique way. Some people feel things very bodily, some less so. Some have a lot of images, others have mainly words. Some find the process very different, others say it is something they often do naturally.

The Four Phases of Focusing

Further light on "experiencing" as a therapeutic process is provided by Gendlin's earlier description of focusing in four phases. The description of these four phases (direct reference, unfolding, global application, and referent movement), complements the approach presented in the six steps.

1. Direct Reference (First Phase)

In this initial phase of focusing (which is roughly analogous to the formulation of Steps 2 and 3), the person directly refers to present, concretely felt, but conceptually vague experiencing. Gendlin offers the example of a hypothetical man in therapy:

> Let us say he has been discussing some troublesome situation or personal trait. He has described various events, emotions, opinions, and interpretations. Perhaps he has called himself "foolish," "unrealistic," and assured his listener that he really "knows better" than to react the way he does. He is puzzled by his own reactions, and he disapproves of them. Or, what amounts to the same thing, he strongly defends his reactions

against some real or imaginary critic who would say that the reactions make no sense, are self-defeating, unrealistic, and foolish. If he is understandingly listened to and responded to, he may be able to refer directly to the felt meaning which the matter has for him. He may then lay aside, for a moment, all his better judgment or bad feeling about the fact that he is as he is, and he may refer directly to the felt meaning of what he is talking about. He may then say something like: "Well, I know it makes no sense, but in some ways it does." Or: "It's awfully vague to me what this is with me, but I feel it pretty definitely." It may seem as if language and logic are insufficient, but the trouble is merely that we are not used to talking about something which is conceptually vague, but definitely and distinctly <u>felt</u>.[36]

As he begins to focus, he may use words like "this" or "this way I feel" as a way for him and the therapist to point to what he is concretely experiencing. Even when the present feeling is very vague, both he and the therapist can use words to directly refer to it.

As the client comes to symbolize his present feeling as "frightening" or "silly" or "terrible," it should be pointed out that it is not an emotion he is attending to but the complex circumstances and personal aspects he feels in his present situation. If the client feels emotion (anger, for example), he can let the emotion subside a bit to sense the broader context of the underlying situation from which the emotion arises. It is the felt sense of the present situation, which underlies the emotion, that the client attends to in direct reference.

Often in the first phase, the person becomes excited or amazed that he can focus on himself in this way. He begins to value this kind of process because it "feels good" even though "what's there" and "where it's all going" are still not very clear. There is a sense of rightness in the process, a kind of relief, and often a lessening of anxiety.

2. Unfolding (Second Phase)

Sometimes in focusing on directly felt experiencing there is a kind of step-by-step coming to know
explicitly what it is. There is an opening up, an
unfolding, which may be quite sudden and dramatic or
may be slow and gradual. Again, Gendlin describes a
typical kind of unfolding that may be experienced:

> Yes, of course he is afraid, he realizes.
> He has not permitted himself even to think
> about dealing with this and this aspect of
> the situation, and this has been because he
> has not believed that these aspects really
> existed. Well, yes, he did realize they
> existed, but he also felt compelled to blame
> himself for them as if he really imagined
> them. And if they do exist (and they do), he
> does not know how he could possibly live with
> them. He has not allowed himself to try to
> deal with them (he now realizes) or even to
> consider them anything other than merely his
> imagination, because, my God, if they are
> really there; then he is helpless. Then
> there is nothing he can do! But they are
> there. Well, it is a relief to know at least
> that.[37]

This example shows the multiplicity to be found in
any felt meaning, in any vague "this" that can be
directly referred to. In the unfolding of the direct
referent, there is usually a surprising and deeply felt
recognition of the good sense of the feeling. "'Of
course,' we say over and over, 'of course!' Or, we say
'Well, what do you know, that's what that was!'"[38]
There is a sense of relief, even though what is symbolized may seem terrible or unsolvable.

As the unfolding occurs, a kind of change is taking place which is more basic than the solution to a
specific problem.

. . . when a direct referent of experienc-

66

ing "opens up," much more change has occurred than the cognitive realization of this or
that. This is most dramatically evident
when, after the "unfolding," the individual
still sees no way out. He says, "At least I
know what it is now, but how will I ever
change it or deal with it?" Yet, during the
following days and in the next therapy hour,
it turns out that he is already different,
that the quality of the problem has changed
and his behavior has been different. And, as
for a good explanation of all this resolution, "well, it just seems all right now."[39]

3. Global Application (Third Phase)

Sometimes, in the moments which immediately follow
the unfolding of a direct referent, the person is
flooded by "many different associations, memories,
situations, and circumstances, all in relation to the
felt referent."[40] These come from the same felt meaning, and yet they may be about different and unrelated
matters. Typically, the person may say:

"Oh, and that's also why I can't get up
any enthusiasm for this-and-this." "Yes, and
another thing about it is, this comes in
every time someone tells me what to do or
think. I can't say, well, what I think is
more important, because, see, this way of
making myself wrong comes in there." "Oh,
and also, back when this and this happened, I
did the same thing."[41]

Often, the person is silent in this third phase.
The change which occurs is global, but all the different applications need not be made explicitly.

One can be sure that for every relation or
application the individual here explicitly
thinks, there are thousands which he does not
think of, but which have, nevertheless, just
changed. Not his thinking about the difference which the unfolding has made, but the
unfolding itself, changes him in all these

67

thousands of respects. The change occurs whether of not he thinks of any such applications, and whether or not he considers the unfolding to be a resolving.[42]

4. Referent Movement (Fourth Phase)

After the three phases of focusing just described, a movement or shift in the experiencing is usually felt, and what the person can now directly refer to in experiencing has changed.

Usually direct reference alone does not change or move the direct referent, but does make it stronger, sharper, and more distinctly felt. It increases its intensity as a feeling and diminishes the diffuse tension, discomfort and anxiety. However, sometimes the mere process of continuous direct reference will change or "move" the direct referent. More often, such a movement occurs after at least some unfolding and symbolizing, and especially after the felt flooding of global application.[43]

While there may appear to be no solution to the problem, in effect, the problem has changed in that the meaning of the whole situation has changed. This changed meaning of the experiencing or changed felt referent Gendlin calls "referent movement."

With this movement, the process has come full cycle. Referent movement is the "completion" of the experiencing process, which provides at the same time a new direction from which it can continue or begin again.

b) The Interpersonal Response and the Manner of Experiencing

A person, says Gendlin, develops in an interpersonal, cultural, and linguistic environment. In fact, "the individual is cultural, social, and interpersonal before he is an individual."[44] In reviewing Martin Heidegger's What Is a Thing?, he observes:

Not only the other people of past history but the other people of now are already an inherent part of what a person is. One is always a being with and a being towards others, and human situations are not possible without this.[45]

Experiencing is interpersonally and culturally patterned. Language is learned only in the context of personally meaningful interaction and then can be used in interaction with present experiencing.[46]

The Interpersonal Response

In therapy, the interpersonal dimension of experiencing is extremely significant. Gendlin believes that successful psychotherapy of any type involves at its core the interpersonal encounter.[47] The reason is that any genuine relationship facilitates a new and different experiential process.

We know, but currently find it hard to investigate or explain, why the client's change and improvement depend so largely upon the interpersonal relationship with the therapist. This is really what changes him, for alone he can think about the same things, yet he remains as he is. We can account for this only if we notice (as we easily can in our own experience and in observations) how different is the experiencing of an individual in a relationship with another, than it is when he is alone, and also, how there are differences in his manner of experiencing in different relationships. I may say and think the same given content under these different circumstances, but my experiencing along with this content will be widely different. My sense of you, the listener, affects my experiencing as I speak, and your response partly determines my experiencing a moment later. What occurs to me, and how I live as we speak and interact, is vitally affected by every word and motion you make, and by every facial expression and attitude you show.[48]

Paying attention to the process of change, Gendlin continues:

> It is not really a matter of what I think you feel about me. Much more, I am affected even without stopping to notice it by every response you give me. I experience your responses. I may come away thinking that, in my opinion, you can feel little liking for me, yet my whole experiential life in the time I spent with you will have been affected not by this opinion of mine, but by our moment-to-moment behaviors which you helped make, which were part of my experiencing as I spoke, thought, felt, and was. Thus it is not the case that I tell you about me, and then we figure out how I should change, and then somehow I do it. Rather, I am changing as I talk and think and feel, for your responses are every moment part of my experiencing, and partly affect, produce, symbolize, and interact with it. And only by this experiencing process (and the difference you make in its character) do I change.[49]

In psychotherapy there is "all the difference between how one thinks and feels alone and how one thinks and feels with another person."[50] The conceptual content may seem, at lest for a time, to be the same either alone or with another, but soon, in an interpersonal context, "the manner of the experiencing will be totally different."[51]

The Manner of Experiencing

In relation to the interpersonal response Gendlin uses the phrase "manner of experiencing" to describe the quality of experiencing's "ongoingness." For example, experiencing may have a certain immediacy or presentness in which the person is alive and at the center of what is being experienced, or it may be so lifeless and dried up that one may feel: "Life is going on all right, but I'm in some back room. I merely hear about it, I'm not living it."[52] Or to put it another way, a person's concrete experiencing may have a "host

riential valuing process actually occurs:

> The order in which experiential valuing
> occurs is the reverse of how it is so often
> portrayed. We do not first adopt value-
> conclusions from some system and then apply
> them to choose between different possibili-
> ties. First we must confront and differenti-
> ate experienced meanings (felt meanings).
> Then we find that these now differentiated
> felt meanings have a significant feel of good
> or bad, resolved or conflicted. If the lat-
> ter, we resolve them by differentiating still
> further and further. For any meaningful
> problem many steps are required, many
> instances of "direct reference," "unfolding,"
> and "referent movement." The seeming inter-
> polated value-direction may shift many times.
> The process has its own direction, its own
> concrete referent which is "next" for it, and
> the felt meanings have their own inward feel
> of resolution or conflict, constriction or
> relief, resentment or freeing, fresh realness
> or stuffy, isolated autism, and just plain
> good or bad.[65]

The direction of experiencing is not based on or
determined by "values." Rather, the reverse is true.
It is the experiencing and its felt differentiation
which determines the direction of the valuing process
and the _actual_ "values" the person comes to hold.

In relating the experiencing process to value-
conclusions, Gendlin makes an important distinction.
There are, he says, "(1) value-conclusions adopted
without an experiential process from which they could
arise; and (2) value-conclusions adopted from an experiential process leading to them."[66]

Within the first kind of value-conclusions, that
is, those not arising from an experiential process,
Gendlin makes another distinction which, as will be
seen, has direct application to religious valuing:

> (1a) Value conclusions without an expe-

75

riential process leading to them can be adopted in a sense which inclines one to readiness to experience what the conclusions imply. In this trouble-free form of 1, the individual expects to experience some day what the value-conclusions involve. This expectation makes him more able to perceive the relevant, rather than other, equally valid, meanings in such experiencing, should it arise. The expectation also makes him more willing to give time, patience, and repeated trials to opportunities for such relevant experiences. In all these ways, influence type 1a succeeds in making it more likely that the individual will, at some time, arrive at the experiential concreteness of the values he has verbally adopted.[67]

The absence of an experiential process can be experienced, however, in a wholly different way:

(1b) Value-conclusions can be adopted without the experiential process leading to them, but accompanied by experiences of confusion, denial, conflict, and surrender of certain areas of enterprise. Such an adoption usually makes it less likely that the individual will ever obtain the experiential process leading to these values, than that he will arrive experientially at other values. It has a thousand side effects, including the predictable behavior differences involved in attempting to act as though he really had the given values, along with failure consequences, conflicts or inferiority, abasement, and resentment.[68]

Value-conclusions, much like the concepts conveying them, can have at least a possible experiential base, or they can exist as separated from the process of experiencing. The verbal meaning of these value-conclusions may be the same in either case, but their function in the ongoing experiencing of the person may be very different.

c) The Experiencing Process as Directional

From the perspective of the primacy of "process" in relation to "content" and especially from the perspective of the "valuing process" in relation to "value-conclusions," it is clear that Gendlin sees the direction of the experiencing process as coming from within the process itself.

In the process of focusing, what Gendlin calls the "focal center" of the process is a function of what was previously felt and symbolized, and each new "focal center" arises as present experiencing is again symbolized and carried forward. In other words, what comes next is determined by the experiencing process itself, as it is ongoing. Gendlin points out:

> The steps of a therapeutic process cannot be determined either by the therapist or by the patient. No prior logical decision can lead it. A perfectly right interpretation may be confusing at one point and helpful at a later point. What comes now is what must come now, what is next for the organism. By carrying forward what is implicit now, a different next step is able to come up later.[69]

Gendlin speculates as to whether there is any common direction to the process of experiencing, that is, whether the continuously shifting value direction of an individual will ultimately lead toward universal values. As he phrases the question: "Is it the case that a great many kinds of value-conclusions are never the result of this experiential process? Is it the case that only certain kinds of value-conclusions can result from it?"[70] Gendlin himself is sure that only certain kinds of value-directions can come from the experiencing process, but the way these values are to be described can only be the result of the further investigation of ongoing experiencing.[71]

d) The Experiencing Process as Growth

The concept of "growth" is used sparingly in Gendlin's writings, yet it seems clear that the ongoingness of experiencing is an experientially defined process of growth.

The basic dynamic of a growth process is evident in the process of focusing. There the ability to symbolize or conceptualize directly-referred-to experiencing has the effect of carrying forward the experiencing process.[72] Within the four phases of focusing, there is a bodily felt step or shift of the organism which is a living forward of the person's experiencing, especially as that experiencing is understood as organism-environment or inside-outside. The shift in feeling (the referent movement), is a further living in one's situation. In a series of these steps or shifts, there is an increase in the implicit aliveness of the experiencing process and a resolution of one's problem of living in the present situation. The steps of focusing have "a pro-life direction."[73]

In a negative way, Gendlin's description of neurosis spells out the nature of the process of growth. There are two elements in blocked or structure-bound experiencing: first, the person is faced with a situational difficulty not able to be lived; and second, experiential focusing which could carry the experiencing further in the situation is absent. Experiencing as a process of growth, therefore, entails an ongoing living in one's situations, and where these situations are difficult, a way of living further in them through focusing.

> A step from a felt sense gives an inner stirring--something is glad to move and speak. That is how life-energy feels when it moves "forward." That is how the "pro-life," or forward moving, direction feels, whatever its content may seem to be. You expand, you are more, the energy flows from inside you outward.[74]

78

4. Critical Reflections

Perhaps the most significant contribution Gendlin makes to a phenomenology of feeling is that "feeling" or "experiencing" is not just a concept, but an <u>actual</u> <u>phenomenon</u>. No longer is "feeling" just something we "have" and can talk about, much as we talk about something external like the weather. It is a <u>felt</u> <u>phenomenon</u>, a bodily phenomenon that can be <u>directly referred</u> <u>to</u>. In other words, a phenomenology of feeling need not be <u>distanced</u>; it can be <u>immediate</u> or <u>direct</u>. Words or symbols need not be in the service of <u>pointing at</u> experiencing, as if from the outside. They can come <u>directly out of</u> experiencing to explicate and further the organism's present living.

Gendlin's phenomenology of "experiencing" in its immediacy is, at the same time, the description of a <u>process</u>. It is a process of interaction with words or symbols. Experiencing needs symbols--especially when it is "structure-bound"--to capture it, to complete it, and to carry it forward as a process. From Gendlin's experiential perspective, words or symbols are an interaction with experiencing, and when used in this way, they are part of an ongoing human process of change. James's analogy that feeling and concepts are "two legs" needed for walking is even truer for Gendlin. Feeling and concepts <u>are</u> the walking. They are the ongoing process of experiencing.

"Experiencing" in its immediacy as a process is also the description of therapeutic change. The person <u>is</u> or <u>is meant to be</u>, a process of change and growth. Gendlin describes this therapeutic process, however, as a function of the <u>immediacy</u> of experiencing. A distanced phenomenology of feeling may reveal "feelings," but these tend to be more content-like, emotional, and epiphenomenal than the felt sense of the organism in its environment. When the felt sense is directly referred to in its immediacy, as it is in focusing, then structure-bound aspects loosen and give way to present experiencing, and then existence is more a process of ongoing, fuller, further living in the situation.

The phenomenon of "experiencing" is at once a radically foundational and relational one. It is a kind of "ur-phenomenon," or in James's phrase, "a germ and starting point." As the person's present, felt existence, it is always there functioning implicitly and able to be referred to. As the person's present felt existence, it is always related to situations and to the endless ways those situations can be differentiated. Meaning is rooted in the process of experiencing. Values are rooted in the process of experiencing. Any environment the person lives in is rooted in the process of experiencing.

There is, as one might expect, a similarity between focusing and James's description of the process of unification. James speaks of a conscious striving to change the situation which is followed finally by a need to "let go" and "surrender," so that "the better self in posse" can direct the operation.[75] Gendlin's focusing, though immediate and momentary, has these similar two elements. There is a conscious focusing of attention on the felt sense of the situation, and then there is a giving up of control, so that the organism might bring about the change.

In the practical realm, focusing offers another way of dealing with the problematic, the unresolved, or whatever it is that needs to change. Usually a person "runs away" from uncomfortable situations, hoping they will somehow go away, or the person "sinks into" the problem, getting lost in its complexity. Focusing is a third stance, a middle therapeutic ground between these two ways of relating. It is a way of directly engaging the problem without getting lost in it, a way of being present to the concern without being identified with it. It is a methodology of both immediacy and space, which is also a methodology (etymologically, "the word or form, along the way") of ongoingness and change. Gendlin's research on "experiencing" offers another way to read Tillich's dictum quoted in the "Introduction."

"The place to look is all places, the place to stand is no place at all."[76]

80

ENDNOTES

1   Eugene T. Gendlin, "Experiencing: A Variable in the Process of Therapeutic Change," The American Journal of Psychotherapy, Vol. 15, No. 2, April 1961, p. 237.

2   Eugene T. Gendlin, "Existentialism and Experiential Psychotherapy," Existential Child Therapy: The Child's Discovery of Himself, Clark Moustakas, ed., New York, Basic Books, 1966, p. 227.

3   Eugene T. Gendlin, Experiencing and the Creation of Meaning: A Philosophical and Psychological Approach to the Subjective, New York, Free Press of Glencoe, 1962, p. 31.

4   Eugene T. Gendlin, "Experiential Psychotherapy," Current Psychotherapies, Raymond Corsini, ed., Itasca, Illinois, Peacock, 1973, p. 322.

5   Eugene T. Gendlin, "Neurosis and Human Nature in the Experiential Method of Thought and Therapy," Humanitas, Vol. 3, No. 2, Fall 1967, p. 142.

6   Eugene T. Gendlin, John Beebe III, James Cassens, Marjorie Klein, and Mark Oberlander, "Focusing Ability in Psychotherapy, Personality, and Creativity," Research in Psychotherapy, Vol. 3, John M. Shlien, ed., Washington, D.C., American Psychological Association, 1967, p. 219.

7   Eugene T. Gendlin, "Experiential Explication and Truth," Journal of Existentialism, Vol. 6, No. 22, Winter 1965-66, p. 139.

8   Gendlin, "Experiential Psychotherapy," p. 324. John Dewey, Experience and Nature, Second Edition, New York, Dover, 1958, p. 4a, also makes this point when he says: "it is not experience which is experienced, but nature--stones, plants, animals, diseases, health, temperature, electricity, and so on. Things interacting in certain ways are experience; they are what is experienced."

9   Eugene T. Gendlin, "Focusing," _Psychotherapy:_
    Theory, Research and Practice, Vol. 6, No. 1,
    Winter 1969, p. 8.

10 Gendlin, "Experiential Explication and Truth,"
    p. 135.

11 Gendlin, "Existentialism and Experiential Psycho-
    therapy," p. 225.

12 Eugene T. Gendlin, "The Role of Knowledge in Prac-
    tice," _The Counselor's Handbook,_ Gail F. Farwell,
    Neal R. Gamsky and Philippa Mathieu-Coughlan,
    eds., New York, Intext Educational Publishers,
    1974, p. 284.

13 Eugene T. Gendlin, "Experiential Phenomenology,"
    Phenomenology and the Social Sciences, Vol. 1,
    Maurice Natanson, ed., Evanston, Illinois, North-
    western University Press, 1973, p. 302.

14 Gendlin, "Experiential Psychotherapy," p. 322.

15 _Ibid._, p. 323.

16 Gendlin, "Existentialism and Experiential Psycho-
    therapy," p. 209.

17 Gendlin, _Experiencing and the Creation of Meaning,_
    p. 11. The words "symbol" and "symbolize" have a
    very precise meaning for Gendlin. A "symbol" is
    anything that directly interacts with or "fits"
    experiencing. Most often we use concepts as a way
    of symbolizing or making present experiencing
    explicit, but that can be done by a gesture, an
    image, an action, or an event--through whatever is
    able to capture present experiencing.

18 Gendlin, "Experiencing: A Variable in the Process
    of Therapeutic Change," p. 237.

19 Gendlin, _Experiencing and the Creation of Meaning,_
    p. 46.

20 Gendlin, "Neurosis and Human Nature in the Expe-

riential Method of Thought and Therapy," p. 147.

21 Eugene T. Gendlin, "A Theory of Personality Change," New Directions in Client-Centered Therapy, J. T. Hart and T. M. Tomlinson, eds., Boston, Houghton Mifflin, 1970, p. 140.

22 Gendlin, "Focusing," p. 5.

23 Eugene T. Gendlin, "Values and the Process of Experiencing," The Goals of Psychotherapy, Alvin R. Mahrer, ed., New York, Appleton-Century-Crofts, 1967, p. 189.

24 Gendlin, "Existentialism and Experiential Psychotherapy," p. 236.

25 Eugene T. Gendlin, "The Discovery of Felt Meaning," Language and Meaning, James B. Macdonald and Robert R. Leeper, eds., Washington, D.C., National Education Association, 1966, p. 47.

26 Gendlin, Experiencing and the Creation of Meaning, p. 5-6.

27 Eugene T. Gendlin, "Experiencing and the Nature of Concepts," The Christian Scholar, Vol. 46, No. 3, Fall 1963, p. 251-252.

28 Gendlin, "Existentialism and Experiential Psychotherapy," p. 221-222.

29 Gendlin, "Experiential Phenomenology," p. 307.

30 Gendlin, "Experiencing and the Nature of Concepts, p. 247.

31 Gendlin, Experiencing and the Creation of Meaning, especially Chapter 3.

32 Gendlin, "A Theory of Personality Change," p. 134.

33 For different descriptions of the six steps, see Eugene T. Gendlin, Focusing, New York, Everest House, 1978, p. 48-49; Eugene T. Gendlin, Focus-

ing, Bantam, 1981, p. 43-64; Eugene T. Gendlin, "How I Teach Focusing--1979," mimeographed, p. 1-16; Eugene T. Gendlin, "A Focusing Intensive Workshop," (four audio tapes), The Focusing Institute and Terra Nova Films, Inc., 1983; Eugene T. Gendlin, _Experiential_ _Psychotherapy_, manuscript for publication, no date, p. 98-103.

34 Gendlin, "How I Teach Focusing--1979," p. 10.

35 A list of people who can help with "focusing," is in the "Directory," in _Focusing_, (the 1981, Bantam edition), p. 171-176.

36 Gendlin, "A Theory of Personality Change," p. 142.

37 _Ibid._, p. 145.

38 _Ibid._

39 _Ibid._

40 _Ibid._, p. 146.

41 _Ibid._, p. 146-147.

42 _Ibid._, p. 147.

43 _Ibid._

44 Gendlin, "Neurosis and Human Nature in the Experiential Method of Thought and Therapy," p. 141.

45 Eugene T. Gendlin, "Analysis," Martin Heidegger, _What_ _Is_ _a_ _Thing_? W. B. Barton, Jr., and Vera Deutsch, trans., Chicago, Regnery, 1967, p. 286.

46 Gendlin, "Values and the Process of Experiencing," p. 190.

47 Gendlin, "Existentialism and Experiential Psychotherapy," p. 213.

48 Gendlin, _Experiencing_ _and_ _the_ _Creation_ _of_ _Meaning_, p. 38.

49 <u>Ibid</u>., p. 38-39.

50 Gendlin, "A Theory of Personality Change," p. 152.

51 <u>Ibid</u>.

52 <u>Ibid</u>., p. 153.

53 <u>Ibid</u>.

54 <u>Ibid</u>., p. 153-154.

55 <u>Ibid</u>., p. 154.

56 Gendlin, "Neurosis and Human Nature in the Experiential Method of Thought and Therapy," p. 143.

57 Gendlin, "A Theory of Personality Change," p. 155.

58 <u>Ibid</u>.

59 Gendlin, <u>Experiential Psychotherapy</u>, p. 18.

60 <u>Ibid</u>.

61 <u>Ibid</u>., p. 158.

62 Gendlin, "The Role of Knowledge in Practice," p. 277.

63 Gendlin, "Experiential Psychotherapy," p. 337.

64 Gendlin, "Values and the Process of Experiencing," p. 181.

65 <u>Ibid</u>., p. 185.

66 <u>Ibid</u>., p. 196.

67 <u>Ibid</u>.

68 <u>Ibid</u>., p. 196-197.

69 Eugene T. Gendlin, "Experiential Psychotherapy," <u>Current Psychotherapies</u>, Second Edition, Raymond

Corsini, ed, Itasca, Illinois, Peacock, 1979, p 342. It is not that the experiencing process is without logical connections, but that its logic is implicit in the unfolding process and can only be really understood retrospectively as the steps of the process are traced back. See Gendlin, <u>Experiential Psychotherapy</u>, p. 42.

70 Gendlin, "Values and the Process of Experiencing," p. 187.

71 <u>Ibid.</u>, p. 189.

72 For an explicit description of growth which is "strongly influenced" by Gendlin's thinking, see Sidney M. Jourard, "Growing Experience and the Experience of Growth," Chapter 13, <u>Disclosing Man to Himself</u>, New York, Van Nostrand Reinhold, 1968, p. 152-172.

73 Gendlin <u>Experiential Psychotherapy</u>, p. 41.

74 Eugene T. Gendlin, <u>Let Your Body Interpret Your Dreams</u>, Wilmette, Illinois, Chiron Publications, 1986, p. 54.

75 William James, <u>The Varieties of Religious Experience</u>, Cambridge, Harvard University Press, 1985, p. 173.

76 Paul Tillich, <u>Systematic Theology</u>, Vol. I, New York, Harper & Row, 1967, p. 26.

CHAPTER THREE

RELIGIOUS EXPERIENCING,

RELIGIOUS GROWTH, EXPERIENTIAL RELIGION,

AND PRACTICAL IMPLICATIONS

This chapter begins with a description of "religious experiencing" which is rooted in the thinking of James and Gendlin. This description leads to an understanding of "religious experiencing" as inherently a process of growth and to three statements which characterize experiential religion. The chapter closes by exploring the implications of "religious experiencing" for religious education, pastoral counseling, and spiritual direction.

1. A Basic Description of Religious Experiencing

What is "religious experiencing?" It is a phenomenon which can be paid attention to directly. As something primary which symbols and concepts can explicate and carry forward, it lives in the person as presently felt. In essence, it is a bodily-felt-relating to the divine (broadly defined). Finally, it is, or at least can be, an unfolding process of the person, a process which is living and changing.

a) Religious Experiencing as a Presently Felt Phenomenon Which Can Be Directly Referred To

The first thing to say about "religious experiencing" is that it is primary, felt, and can be paid attention to directly. It exists for the person as a felt phenomenon, as something actually there in present bodily living. For the person who is in relation to God, this relation in its primacy is presently lived and bodily felt.

As an experientially irreducible phenomenon, "religious experiencing" is primary because it does not present itself as something derived from other feelings or concepts. Concepts and symbols come from it and help refer back to it. "Religious experiencing" as a presently felt phenomenon has primacy in respect to the words or symbols we use to pay attention to it.

At any time one can directly refer to the present sense of how things are in relation to God. He or she can ask inwardly: "How am I with God right now? What am I feeling now in the way I am with God?" If one can wait for a moment, perhaps some felt sense will form which can be referred to. At first, for example, it may be a very vague sense of easing. In time, words may come like: "There's a sense of comfort there." Already some words are coming from the present feeling to say what it is. If the person continues to pay attention to the felt phenomenon of "religious experiencing," perhaps more words or an image will come. One might say: "It's like somehow it's all O.K., God is with me." As one continues to focus on religious experiencing, it may unfold still more with new words coming from it. This focusing is possible because "religious experiencing" is a primary, present, felt phenomenon which can be directly referred to.

James and Gendlin

Of all the contributions James's thinking makes to "religious experiencing," the most significant is his emphasis on the primacy of "feeling" over "conceptualization." For James, "feeling" is the essence of religion, the "very citadel of human life."[1] It is primitive, unreflective, non-rational, subconscious and the "real thing" in us. It is feeling that has the depth. In concrete feeling we have "fact in the making."[2] According to James, concepts and theological formulas are only "secondary products," consequent upon and not independent of primary feeling.[3] In fact, they "depend on primary feeling for their very existence."[4]

88

There can be no question that Gendlin's phenomenology leads him to an equal emphasis on the primacy of feeling. "Experiencing" is a kind of "ur-phenomenon," a primal matrix out of which symbols and concepts as well as explicit meanings and values arise. Experiencing itself is preconceptual, yet because it is implicitly meaningful it guides conceptualization. In Gendlin's words, experiencing is "primary in that some explicit meanings may 'fit' it and some may not."[5]

While James is clearly interested in the individual who "feels the presence of the living God,"[6] while he is able to detail his own generalized sense of the divine, and while in the Principles he describes feeling as the "germ and starting point" for thought,[7] still in the Varieties the primacy of religious feeling he describes is somewhat distanced. He speaks of a feeling which is very content-like, very much like concepts, only non-conceptual. James is not consistent in presenting feeling as a underlying process of felt existence.[8] With his notion of "experiencing" Gendlin allows "religious experiencing" to be seen clearly as a living phenomenon. Religious feeling can be defined not just as certain contents in the person, but more basically as an underlying, preconceptual, implicitly meaningful process of the person's bodily living and interacting.

Like any other aspect of experiencing, "religious experiencing" can always be directly referred to and can, perhaps, be adequately symbolized. In other words, if one has a felt relation to the divine, the relationship is implicitly meaningful and can, at least theoretically, be symbolized and made explicit. It is, of course, only the symbolization of "religious experiencing" which ultimately differentiates or marks out such experiencing as religious. Yet what is primarily the religious is not the symbolization but the underlying, felt experiencing of the divine. This phenomenon is "religious experiencing."

b) Religious Experiencing as a Felt Relating to the Divine

"Religious experiencing" is a relating to the

divine, but a relating which primarily exists in feeling. Both elements are important: "religious experiencing" is a <u>felt</u> relating, a <u>felt</u> interacting, a <u>felt</u> response, and this felt relating is <u>to the divine</u>. "Religious experiencing" <u>is</u> the relating to God in its present livingness.

There are general ways in which people formally <u>know</u> that they are related to God, as creatures, for example, or as redeemed. It seems, however, that many people are often unaware of the <u>felt sense</u> of how they are presently relating to God (which is also a kind of knowing). A woman may say, for example, that she knows she is loved by God, yet if she were to focus on the present felt relationship, she might find that she feels rejected by God, not loved at all.

"Religious experiencing" as a present <u>felt</u> relating to the divine may, at first, not be very clear at all. Gradually as the felt sense begins to form, it will be unique for each person in the present moment with many implicit aspects or textures to it which might be differentiated and made explicit. It may be a sense of absence or a sense of presence. It may be felt as challenging, affirming, judging, or supporting. It may have an intimate sense to it, or it may be characterized by a sense of mystery or power. It may contain a deep sense of happiness or security, and it may not. In short, the felt relating to the divine is just what it is in the moment, and it changes as the person continues to live his or her relationship to the divine.

The "divine" in religious experiencing may be represented in any number of changing ways. It may be an objective, transcendent God who acts and responds. It may be the mystery within sacred time and space. It may be the depth revealed in an interpersonal sharing of love and hope. It may be the coalescing dynamic of a universe striving for fulfillment. The images of God are as varied as those who have them, from the "gentle breeze" of Elijah to the "beauty ever ancient, ever new" of Augustine, to the "present God" of Brother Lawrence, to the "Thou" of Martin Buber, "the God of love and affliction" of Simone Weil, and even the "Unstared

Stare" of Jean-Paul Sartre.

Often the meaning of the divine may be difficult to clearly conceptualize at all. It may be definitely felt, but the words that would make it explicit may be so general or so trite as to be almost wholly inadequate. It may have much to do with a certain place, but the felt significance of that may defy articulation. It may have something to do with an event, a season, or a time of the year. It may have to do with a certain community or with the kind of sharing which breaks into transcendence. If the meaning of the divine can be felt as objective, it can also be felt as situated or contextual--and there may be no vocabulary at all to differentiate and symbolize the implicit meaning.

James and Gendlin

The phenomenology which allows James to see feeling as primary in religion also allows him to see feeling and its object or referent interwoven within the one experience or event. For James, religious feeling is of the divine. There is no separation or dichotomy of feeling in the immediacy of religious experience. The religious feelings that James describes are almost always in terms of the "sense of presence" of the divine. He defines the divine as "a primal reality" which the person "feels impelled to respond to."[9] The feeling response in religion is in relation to the "divinity of the object."[10] And he points out: "As the sense of real presence of these objects fluctuates, so the believer alternates between warmth and coldness in his faith."[11]

Since for James the divine is an experiential object defined by each person, religious feeling is always a response to the way the divine is experienced. He insists that the divine be understood broadly as "any object that is godlike, whether it be a concrete deity or not."[12] Just as there is "no one specific and essential kind of religious object," so there is "no one elementary religious emotion, but only a common storehouse of emotions upon which religious objects may draw."[13] Religious feelings are normal feelings, specified in the relating to their divine referent.

While Gendlin does not speak of a felt relating to the divine, he shows that experiencing is always situated, always in interaction with the environment. If the divine can be sensed as part of the environment, then it is easy to speak of a felt relation to the divine. In describing experiencing with respect to a person's situation, Gendlin also puts a great deal of emphasis on the response coming from another. Gendlin's thinking lets us see the interpersonal "other" as very important, not only for transmitting the types and nuances of religious meaning in the culture, but also for sharing what personal religious meaning might surface in interpersonal experiencing.

In contrast to Gendlin's emphasis on the interpersonal dimension of experiencing, much of James's description of the feeling response in religion is in terms of a private event. He pays little attention to the interpersonal dimension of the event, e.g., the suggestion coming from another, the speaker at the temperance meeting, or the words of Scripture. Nor does he focus on the broader communal and cultural contexts in which the religious event may be situated or on other factors which may lead to it. With Gendlin's perspective it can be said that "religious experiencing" is always, at least implicitly, situated and environmental. There will always be a cultural matrix within which the divine is experienced, and the individual's present situation will enter into this experiencing as well. Most immediately, the interpersonal context, especially personal responses from others to one's present felt experiencing, may have a marked influence on how "religious experiencing" functions.

In summary, it can be said, on the one hand, that the "religious experiencing" of the individual is always in some relation to the divine. On the other hand, this "divine" is to be broadly conceived as an experiential reality, in which the individual's cultural, situational, and interpersonal living and interacting is involved. The referent of the felt process of "religious experiencing" can be described by the word "contextual" as well as by the word "objective."

c) Religious Experiencing as Implicitly Meaningful and as Needing Symbols or Concepts to Explicate It

There is meaning in "religious experiencing." That is to say, the experiencing carries its own sense of significance, its own valuing. The meaning there for the person in "religious experiencing" is, however, a felt meaning which is essentially implicit. In other words, there is meaning which is definitely felt but which, initially at least, may not yet be symbolically brought to awareness. Words, images, or actions are necessary to capture and bring into awareness the meaning already implicitly there in "religious experiencing." What is primarily the religious is not the words or symbols but the underlying, felt, organismic, implicitly meaningful experiencing of the divine, that is, the phenomenon of "religious experiencing."

In a typical kind of "religious experiencing" a person may begin to pay attention to the felt way he or she is with God. It seems to be "something," and, staying with the feeling, the person may say: "It's not clear, but it feels like scared of something . . . I don't know." And then, in a minute: "I'm afraid of God . . . I don't trust God . . . It's almost like I don't trust myself." Perhaps with more focusing on the present feeling, words might come like: "It's just too hard." And then, in a moment, the person might smile and say: "I fight God instead of fighting myself." With that there is a sigh, a sense of relief, indicating that the felt meaning of "religious experiencing" is now sufficiently explicated. In this example the implicit meaning of "religious experiencing" needs words to explicate and carry it forward, yet the "religious experiencing" itself guides the choice of words which are right. The concepts touch traditional religious themes of fear and trust in God, but here they are used experientially as they make tracks into the rich, undifferentiated complexity of the actually lived situation in order to form and explicate it.

James and Gendlin

Although the idea that "religious experiencing" is implicitly meaningful and needs symbols of some kind to

93

be explicated is clearly drawn from Gendlin's thinking, it is by no means foreign either in James's Varieties or in his other writings. The noetic quality of religious feeling is a theme played with many variations in the Varieties. James speaks of religious feelings as "genuine perceptions of truth"[14] and "fact in the making."[15] Within the "feeling-conceptualization" contrast he says quite clearly that "articulate reasons are cogent for us only when our inarticulate feelings of reality have already been impressed in favor of the same conclusion."[16] Later in the Varieties when discussing those who have experienced self-surrender, he observes: "They know; for they have actually felt the higher powers . . ."[17] Running throughout the Varieties is the equation of primary feeling with an equally primary sense of knowledge and truth.

Some of the more direct phenomenology of James's other writings surfaces an equally clear sense of an inchoate knowing which resides in feeling. In the Principles, for example, he calls feelings "vague cognizers of the same realities which other conscious states cognize and name exactly."[18] He also points to an implicit truth in feeling when he remarks: "the state of the feeling and the state of naming the feeling are continuous, and the infallibility of such prompt introspective judgments is probably great."[19]

Gendlin's thinking gives even greater clarity to James's direct phenomenology. All feeling is meaningful, but it is meaningful as felt. "Experiencing" is of felt, implicit meaning which, when focused on, can open up and change as symbols come to say explicitly what it is. For "religious experiencing" this means that the felt relation to the divine is a present and continuing process which always has meaning. This meaning can be available to the person, if, through focusing, "religious experiencing" guides the words or symbols being used.

d) Religious Experiencing as a Process Which Is Able to Unfold

This fourth aspect of "religious experiencing," including as it does the other aspects just described, shows "religious experiencing" as <u>inherently</u> a <u>process</u> <u>which</u> <u>is</u> <u>able</u> <u>to</u> <u>unfold</u>. When it is directly referred to, the implicit meaning of the felt relating to the divine is able to be explicated in a way that brings with it an unfolding of the "religious experiencing" itself.

Just how is "religious experiencing" a process of the person? To begin with, it can be process as part of the over-all bodily-felt-livingness of the person, and in this sense it is in process with the changing events, situations, and interactions of day-to-day living. For example, a woman brought up as a child to feel God was "spying on me all the time" had a sense of God as "wrathful" and "punishing." A number of years later, and after being in counseling, she realized that her sense of God had changed. Her way of describing the new sense of God was: "I think maybe God's a swell guy." Her "religious experiencing" was in process with the rest of her living and changing over the years.[20]

Looking more directly at the phenomenon of "religious experiencing" itself, one finds that what constitutes it as a process is that it reveals itself as a flow of felt meaning in relation to the divine. It is a changing felt sense in relating to God, and one can know it as such by dipping into the flow, as it were, and extracting a content. One can pay attention to the present felt meaning and with appropriate words or images see the explicit meaning which is there. The religious "content," the explicit religious meaning, is itself an aspect of the process, a capturing of the flow.

A still fuller sense of "religious experiencing" as process is had when it can be focused on continuously. In other words, "religious experiencing" is realized as a process most completely through the procedure of experiential focusing. Through focusing a person directly refers to it, thereby engendering a process of unfolding. Quintessentially, then, "religious experiencing" is process as <u>the</u> <u>unfolding</u> <u>of</u> <u>the</u> <u>implicit</u> <u>meaning</u> <u>in</u> <u>the</u> <u>relating</u> <u>to</u> <u>the</u> <u>divine</u>. This unfolding is a furthering or deepening of the flow of the felt meaning of ongoing relating to God. Brought about through focusing, it is a change in the quality or manner of felt relating. While there is no research yet to show the exact nature of this change, this writer's observations suggest that often a person feels freer, more hopeful, and more alive in relating to God, while the sense of God often seems to be clearer and less distant. In short, for some at least, there seems to be an increased sense of relating which moves toward harmony or unity--interestingly enough, some of the characteristics of the process of conversion described by James.

James and Gendlin

Although the contribution James's thinking makes to an understanding of "religious experiencing" as a process is neither as immediate nor as useful as Gendlin's, it is one of pioneering insight and corroborative value nonetheless. In the Varieties, James suggests a definite connection between religious feeling and conversion. He speaks of conversion as a process whereby "dead feelings" become "live ones."[21] He describes self-surrender to the higher power as a "native hardness" which must "break down and liquify."[22] He even sees some direction in feeling as a process when, speaking of conversion, he remarks that when "the subconscious forces take the lead, it is more probably the better self in posse which directs the operation."[23]

In the Principles, James clearly describes feeling as a process. He speaks of feelings of relation as "an unbroken stream," saying that every image in the mind is "steeped and dyed in the free water that flows round it."[24] He also remarks that perceptual experience is "naturally a flux" which can never be superseded.[25] In Some Problems of Philosophy, he approaches experiencing as an ongoing process when he says: "Percepts and concepts interpenetrate and melt together, impregnate and fertilize each other. Neither, taken alone, knows reality in its completeness. We need them both, as we need both our legs to walk with."[26]

The contribution of Gendlin's thinking to an understanding of "religious experiencing" as a process

96

is immediate and invaluable. "Experiencing" is existence as a felt living and interacting. It is the felt meaning of the person in his or her situations. It is implicit in that it is always there functioning as meaning, but often the meaning is not yet symbolized so that the person knows what it is. When one is able to focus on experiencing, the meaning can open up or unfold; words or images come to explicate it; experiencing is carried forward as an ongoing organism-environment process.

In this elaboration of a fourfold description of "religious experiencing" through James and Gendlin, two related points need to be kept in mind. The first point is that in many ways their contributions to a process understanding of religious experience are complementary, even though the thinking of Gendlin is often presented as a way of clearly achieving some of the things that the thinking of James is only intimating. The main contribution of James to "religious experiencing" is his rooting of religion in individual feeling. The main contribution of Gendlin to "religious experiencing" is his understanding of experiencing as inherently a situated, interpersonal, unfolding process. The common and operative and integrative phenomenon that both James and Gendlin focus on is "feeling." James talks of this feeling basically in terms of contents in respect to a religious object. Gendlin talks of this feeling as an ongoing process of change and growth. Their shared phenomenological approach to "feeling," however, allows for a useful interplay of their observations as brought to bear on "religious experiencing."

The second point is that, while the resources in James and Gendlin are relied upon to articulate "religious experiencing" as an aspect of the experiencing process, the over-riding concern here is not simply to show the compatibility of their thinking. The primary concern of this book is to locate and describe an actual phenomenon which is "in" or "of" the person. At the heart of religious experience is a living, concrete, observable phenomenon which can be directly referred to, symbolized, and allowed to unfold.

2. Religious Experiencing and Growth

The possibility of being able to speak in a foundational way of "religious experiencing" in relation to growth lies in the fact that "religious experiencing" is a dimension of the person's concrete experiencing process and in the fact that this experiencing--when able to be accurately and continuously symbolized--is an experientially defined process of growth. In relation to growth, then, the first thing to be said about "religious experiencing" is that, when ongoing and unfolding, it is a growth process. If certain words, events or symbols can interact with "religious experiencing" in such a way as to capture it and carry it forward, then the person is growing religiously.

It is important to point out that religious growth is best seen as a unique dimension of a broader growth process. As James has said, experience of the divine and surrender to the higher power seem to provide for many the wider life, freedom, and charity not easily duplicated by other kinds of experiencing.[27] Religious growth, however, need not be defined in opposition to human growth. If the experiencing process is foundational, then the terms "religious" and "human" can simply be seen as different ways of specifying this process. When symbols, that is, concepts, events, images, or actions, interact with the religious dimension of experiencing and carry it forward, it makes sense to speak of religious growth or growth in terms of the unfolding of "religious experiencing."

The work of James and Gendlin suggests not only that "religious experiencing," when ongoing, is a concrete process of growth but also that this growth is in response "to the divine" or "to God" or "to the higher power." "Religious experiencing" is a relating to the divine; it is an interacting with the higher power as an aspect of one's situations or environment. Religious growth is, therefore, growth in this relating.

Often growth in relating to the divine is understood as growth in the meaning of the divine.[28] It seems, however, that at the heart of a changing meaning of the divine is an ongoing felt experiencing which

98

continuously interacts and which functions as implicit meaning. For growth to take place in respect to "religious experiencing," it is important that, in the interacting with the divine, the implicit meaning be able to become explicit as the felt relating is captured and furthered. Growth in relating to the divine is revealed as felt meaning becomes explicit.

If ongoing "religious experiencing" is a process of growth, it is easy to see that when the process is not ongoing there is an absence of growth. If the manner of "religious experiencing" can be alive, open, fresh in the immediacy of relating to God, the manner may also be blocked, structure-bound or frozen. Ongoing "religious experiencing" exists when the felt meaning of that experiencing functions implicitly and is able to be symbolized or conceptualized. Exactly which symbols can be used to make presently felt "religious experiencing" explicit depends on the individual, the tradition he or she has been raised in, and the situations and events, religious and otherwise, that have been experienced. Most important for growth, however, will be the possibility of focusing on "religious experiencing"--along with the interpersonal response from others which helps in that focusing--in such a way that just the symbolization which has an experiential effect can be found.

There is any number of ways of understanding why a person's "religious experiencing" may not be ongoing. A person has come, perhaps, to a situation with God in which there is no way to move. The religious situation seems unsolvable, and the person is blocked in relating to God because of it.[29] Another person's need for security or stability may be such that a fixed "religious experiencing" may be the only island of safety in an otherwise threatening sea. For another person "religious experiencing" may be so connected to negative experiences in childhood that it effectively becomes blotted out or consciously rejected in the interest of breathing space or survival.[30] For another person religion may be so bound up with the experience of prejudice that any "religious experiencing" may be severely hampered. For another person "religious experiencing" may be blocked because God is so identified with primitive conceptualizations that the concepts themselves effectively block the possibility of any real experiencing.[31] For another person religion may be experienced as in no way connected with life so that whatever "religious experiencing" might occur is not in dialogue with the rest of the experiencing process. For another person psychological development and interpersonal relationships may be so impoverished that blocked experiencing in these areas hinders "religious experiencing" as well. In short, there is any number of possible explanations of "blocked" or "frozen" relating to the divine.

One of the most useful implications of Gendlin"s thinking is that in these religious situations a process of ongoingness or growth may be able to be facilitated through focusing, especially with the help of another who is comfortable with the dimension of "religious experiencing."

A good example of how blocked "religious experiencing" can change and become ongoing is from the focusing session of a woman who finds "something in the way" in her relationship with God.[32] The following is a transcript of the session.

C Let yourself get comfortable, breathe a bit . . . and gently ask yourself: How am I with God right now. What's it like between me and God right now? And don't answer, but wait and see if some kind of feeling comes to say how it is between you and God right now . . . And see if some feeling won't come . . . some sense of what it's like between you and God. And if a lot of words come, see if you can't get down to the feeling level of just how you are right now with God . . . And don't make it be anything. Just let yourself get some felt sense of how you are with God. Let the feeling come, and be gentle with it.

F It's like there's a knot in my stomach.

C Um, so there's a knot there in your stomach, that's what it's like . . . Let yourself pay attention to the knot, and just be there with that . . . and see what it all feels like, that knot in your stomach

. . . And don't analyze it. Just let yourself be with the feeling that's there . . .

F It's a very tense feeling.

C It's very tense. Stay with that. Stay with that tense feeling . . . that knot there in your stomach, and just let it be there . . . and be friendly to it and welcome it . . . Just let yourself stay with the feeling, and don't talk to it. And try not to fight it (she appears to be fighting it) . . . Just let it be there . . . Just let yourself stay there . . .

F It's like the tenseness is spreading. It's more than just in the stomach.

C O.K. . . . the tenseness is spreading and it feels like more than just a knot. Stay with that. Stay with that feeling that you have there very much in your body . . . and be gentle with it, and just let yourself feel it . . .

F It's hard to be gentle with the tenseness.

C Let it be there . . . and see if you can be gentle . . . Just let yourself stay with the feeling. And if you find there's a word that comes, or an image, or something to say what that's like, then see what that is . . . but stay with the feeling that's there.

F It's like a frightened feeling . . . I can feel it in my shoulders . . . definitely.

C So it's a frightened feeling. It's the kind of feeling you can feel yourself tensing up (she is tensing up). Stay with that. Stay with that feeling just the way it is for you . . . And try not to analyze it, and try not to fight it. Just let it be there for you the way it seems to be . . .

F It's like I'm holding on to something and can't let go.

C There's something you're holding on to and you can't let go. Stay with that . . . (inaudible). See if

101

you can get some sense of what it is there you're holding onto and can't let go . . . Just let yourself be with it . . . Stay with the feeling that's there.

F It's kind of like I want God on my terms and not his.

C It's kind of like you want God on your terms and not his. Let yourself feel it. Stay with the feeling that's there.

F I'm still frightened.

C It's not quite right, there's still something wrong. Be patient with it. Stay with that . . . that's not quite right. There's still something wrong. See what that is . . . And don't figure it out. Let yourself get the feel of it, the feel of what that is that still, still something wrong.

F I don't, I don't feel as tense, but I don't feel right . . .

C It's not as tense, but it's still not quite right. Something's there. There's part of it, but there's the sense it's not quite the whole thing. Something's still not quite right . . .

F It's like if, if I let go, I'll get hurt.

C Um hm, O.K., it's like if I let go I'll get hurt . . . Stay with the feeling you have there.

F It's kind of hard not to try to figure out how I'll get hurt.

C Um, not to figure out the feeling that says: I'll get hurt . . . (inaudible) . . . Let yourself stay with that feeling (inaudible).

F And now it's coming back again.

C Um, now it's coming back . . . Let yourself pay attention to it . . . Just be with it . . . and try not to fight it . . . Just be with it.

F The feeling's changing (inaudible).

C Uh, the feeling is changing . . . Let yourself be with whatever's there. Don't make it do anything and try not to make it be anything. Just be with what's there for you.

F Like there's something telling me to let go, but I'm not sure . . . what . . .

C So a sense there . . . there's something telling you to let go, but you're not sure what it is. Stay with the feeling that's there. Try not to figure it out, but just stay with the feeling that you have . . . let it tell you . . .

F Some of the tenseness is going . . . It's my own will and not his (inaudible).

C It's your own will and not his (inaudible), um, stay with that (inaudible).

F (relaxing and smiling) Now I feel good.

C And now you feel good. There's a sense there that it's my own will and not his . . .

F That's it.

This is a good example of what it is like to focus on "religious experiencing" so that it can unfold and become more ongoing. This woman feels there is "something in the way" in her relating to God, but she does not know what it is. By letting herself focus on the felt sense of her relating to the divine, gradually-- and very bodily--it begins to open up. It moves, as focusing often does, from a quality of experiencing ("frightened") to a more explicit unfolding of felt meaning ("It's like I'm holding on to something and can't let go"). And then, almost immediately, more explicit meaning comes ("It's kind of like I want God on my terms and not his"). Some reduction of the tension she feels in relating to God occurs. There is a bodily felt shift, a step in the process, but something is still not quite right.

As she continues to pay attention to her "religious experiencing," more meaning becomes explicit ("It's like if, if I let go, I'll get hurt"). This is interesting new information which she wants to figure out. Instead, she decides to stay with its felt version, which returns almost immediately ("And now it's coming back again"). More meaning unfolds ("Like there's something telling me to let go, but I'm not sure . . . what . . ."). Finally, there is a second step, an unmistakable bodily shift of resolution, and the words come ("It's my own will and not his"). Throughout this whole process, she is moving further or deeper into her living relationship with God, as her "religious experiencing" is carried forward. The focusing facilitates ongoingness, steps of religious change and growth.

It happens that this example of focusing on "religious experiencing" is very much like James's understanding of religious conversion. The process appears to be an incremental version of the more sudden and dramatic conversion experiences recounted in the Varieties. The central content that surfaces as the process of change in "religious experiencing" occurs is expressed in the phrases: "God on my own terms," "to let go," "my own will and not his." James's description of the heart of the process of conversion touches the same theme, that is, letting go, giving up the will, surrendering to the higher power.

In the process of "religious experiencing" any number of symbols and concepts may be used--but only if they interact with the person's present experiencing. These symbols may evolve over the course of one's life, as is the case with James, but they need not be constantly changing. For someone raised in a given tradition they may be the ones used all along, but through focusing the felt meaning of these symbols may change. There may be a deeper meaning in the concepts, reflecting a changed quality of experiencing. Although not speaking in the context of focusing, James Tracy suggests this kind of change when he says:

"I believe Jesus Christ is the incarnate Son of God" uttered by me here and now means much more than the same utterance ten years ago. Though the words remain identical, their meaning for me has deepened and broadened. What evolves, then, is not the proposition but the individual person pronouncing the proposition.[33]

Writing about religious maturity, Orlo Strunk makes much the same point: "Perhaps the beliefs may now be stated in terms exactly as they were communicated to us in childhood, but now the meanings they have are far richer and have taken on an added dimension."[34] One way to understand both these observations is not simply that the meanings are deeper or richer, but that the underlying, implicitly felt "religious experiencing" has been able to flow and unfold over the years, no doubt in the context of communal worship, faith sharing, caring for those in need, and other inner as well as outer practices which touch the felt relationship with God.

A question arises in relation to "religious experiencing" as a process of growth, a question suggested by James's description of the "best fruits" of religion as seen in conversion and saintliness. The question is: Can it be said that "religious experiencing," as an ongoing phenomenon, has a direction? In light of James's description of the fruits of conversion and saintliness and in light of Gendlin's finding that the experiencing process has its own direction, a preliminary answer would seem to be that there is a direction in "religious experiencing." If the feelings that James associates with the outcome of religious conversion, namely "inner unity and peace," and "a characteristic sort of relief,"[35] are taken together with some of the features of saintliness, namely "a willing self-surrender," and "elation and freedom,"[36] and if these feelings are in reality the symbolization of implicit experiencing (from which they come as "contents"), then "religious experiencing" clearly has a direction. Ultimately, of course, this question of direction is an experiential one which can be answered only by a study of those engaged in ongoing "religious experiencing."

Another question arises in reference to the change

that takes place in "religious experiencing." And this question concerns the influence of another person: Does interpersonal experiencing engender "religious experiencing"? One writer who sees a positive connection between the two is James V. Clark. In "Toward a Theory and Practice of Religious Experiencing" he insists that sensitivity training is the most religious enterprise he knows.

> Placed in the environment of one of these groups, people seem, in their own ways, to go through the development of a religion. Although the revelations and the symbols used in each individual's faith and witnessing have their own unique content for each person, the process each person goes through appears similar to the development of any religion.[37] (Emphasis mine)

To point out the way this religious process in engendered, Clark quotes Martin Buber who says that it is "from one man to another that the heavenly bread of self being is passed."[38] The central point he makes in the article is that it is through interpersonal experiencing that religious symbols are experienced:

> . . . the mutually revelatory relation is the medium in which all the central elements of religious experience emerge almost at once. These elements are a revelatory experience, the development of transcendent values such that the person values facing toward the content of his revelation, faith in Tillich's sense of developing an internal ultimate concern with the external ultimate seen only in symbols, and witnessing, by which I mean acting--moving toward or in some way expressing one's ultimate concern.[39]

The process Clark describes here is similar to the manner of experiencing with the help of an interpersonal other described by Gendlin. The emergence of "religious experiencing" seems to be attributable to the process facilitated by the sensitivity trainer. One of the major influences Clark sees as bringing about this process is "the conviction and skill of the professional in designing the experience and helping it unfold."[40]

The dynamics of the interaction with an interpersonal other is described by Clark in light of his own theology:

> To create God's presence is a joy and a duty of each human being . . . It is a joy and duty because we are doing what we need to do for our own creation. When man avoids experiencing himself as a creator, he sins against his own basic nature, and in that sense it is his duty to place himself in relation to the other who is presenting himself. Certainly central points of Buber are that God presents himself through the other and that it takes an I to create a Thou. When another "secretly and bashfully watches for a silent Yes" and when we move toward him and respond to him with our "I-ness," we create him. And if God is presenting Himself through the human other, we create Him.[41]

Clark is obviously drawing from his own group experience in describing interpersonal experience as a process of religious growth. Whether this process is therapeutic, strictly speaking, or whether religious development simply flows out of the depth of this kind of interpersonal encounter, there is no doubt he is proposing an engendering of "religious experiencing" which arises in interpersonal experiencing, an engendering which seems to be as well a process of transcendent valuing.

The "religious experiencing" (and its attendant transcendent valuing) which arises out of deep interpersonal experiencing needs symbolization. Clark insists that this symbolization come from the experiencing, even though the symbols may be part of a religious tradition. Using the language of Tillich, he observes:

> For a person unconditionally to center

himself toward the ultimate, its symbols must
be unreservedly his own. Regardless of its
origin, he must have taken it utterly and
completely into himself, as did the group
members who felt the hands of Christ and who
saw the face of Budda and "Eli." Because the
symbols of religious organization are not our
own originally, we are quite correct (in a
developmental sense) to reject them. And
most intellectuals and professionals have.
Indeed it appears that most people have. But
we are left needing an experience in which we
can develop our own symbols. It may well be
that later on we will see in culturally more
wide-spread symbols, such as that of Christ
on the cross, even deeper and more meaningful
expressions of the object of our ultimate
concern.[42] (Emphasis mine)

Other writers have come to similar conclusions
about the relation of interpersonal experience to religious experience. Clark's findings are viewed here at
some length because the context of his descriptions is
close to Gendlin's "experiencing," because he includes
in his own way some of the basic characteristics of
"religious experiencing" presented in the first section
of this chapter, and because he shows that interpersonal experiencing does seem to engender "religious
experiencing" in the person.

3. A Basic Description of Experiential Religion

From time to time there is a call for a return to
experience in religion. There is criticism of a of
religion that has become too abstract, too impersonal,
too far removed from the way ordinary people seem to
live and construe their feelings in relation to the
divine. Writing with an ecclesial perspective and from
the Baptist tradition, Paul Clifford sees the situation
this way:

The fact is that most people do not feel
that the church really meets them in either
its teaching or its ritual. They have a
sense of a great hiatus which is at a far

deeper level than that of the intellect; it is at the very wellsprings of human life where emotions rule to a degree that most of us simply have not measured. For if emotional response is not evoked by the way in which the faith is articulated, we can be sure that the latter is not being related to any profound intuitive awareness. What is commonplace in psychology has hardly come to the surface in ecclesiastical circles.[43]

Writing within the Roman Catholic tradition, Kilian McDonnell asks:

How is the Church to speak to the unbeliever or even the unbelieving believer about a belief which has nothing to do with experience, with that room in which one experiences one's concrete historical self.[44]

McDonnell goes on to observe that the mistrust of personal religious experience in the Catholic tradition is related to "an exaggerated objectivism" in doctrine and in the sacraments.[45]

This was an objectivism so sophisticated in its defense of the non-personal . . . that it made the possibility of personal piety more than usually difficult. This objectivism, which, of course, played and still rightly plays an important role in Catholic theological thought, pushed the concept of grace back and away from the world where man lives and feels and experiences, pushed it into an objectified spiritual realm beyond man's consciousness, and grace became an unconscious modality of the soul.[46]

From a similar ecclesial context, Morton Kelsey in the Episcopal tradition comments on the need for personal experience in religion:

. . . this new generation, both young and old, are not satisfied with authority; they want experiences of God to verify the theology and the dogma. And this . . . is exactly what the modern church and modern theology are short on, even hostile to.[47]

An understanding of experiential religion can begin to articulate a response to this perceived gap between personal feeling and formal religion. This experiential religion is the result of a shift in perspective on "religious experiencing"--a shift from the way "religious experiencing" functions as an inherent process of growth to the way that this "ur-phenomenon" provides a new way of defining religion itself. Three basic statements characterize experiential religion: a) Experiential religion does not focus on God but on the experiencing of God; b) Experiential religion sees religious symbols, values, and beliefs as interacting with "religious experiencing;" and c) Experiential religion is engendered by interpersonal experiencing and is a manner of experiencing.

a) Experiential religion does not focus on God but on the experiencing of God.

If both James and Gendlin are right in their assertions regarding the primacy of feeling in relation to conceptualization, then in order to speak of God in a personal way, an individual must use words directly related to the feeling process. In "religious experiencing," a person will, of course, reflect the culture and the collective experiencing of the communities to which he or she belongs, yet the concepts which the person uses that have personal meaning will also come from personal experiencing. To speak personally about the divine is to speak out of one's own "religious experiencing."

In experiential religion the focus is on the experiencing of God and not simply on the more objective divine entity that may be revealed in that experiencing. Yet with the influence of the empirical paradigm so operative in scientific knowing, it is easy to see religion as being only about God and to forget that what is usually being considered is the divine as experienced by someone. Most often religious language is understood as saying who God is rather than how God

110

is experienced.

One of the important implications of "religious experiencing" is that a basic distinction can be made between experiential and non-experiential religion. In experiential religion the divine would always be seen as arising concretely from the person's experiencing process, while in non-experiential religion the focus would be on the divine but without explicit reference to personal experiencing. Either approach to religion is possible; religious concepts and symbols can be used in the service of experiential or non-experiential religion. At issue, however, is the meaning of these symbols. Langdon Gilkey characterizes the issue this way:

> . . . theological symbols, explicated without reference to ordinary experience, have meaning only "eidetically" in terms of their inherent structures or intentional meaning. They do not have <u>religious</u> meaning for us, though we who study them may realize emphatically that they have had some such meaning for others. (. . .) The meanings of religious symbols for others are available to us through a careful study of religions, Biblical or otherwise, but one must not confuse an understanding of their eidetic meanings with the religious meaning for us of these symbols in our contemporary situation. That meaning is possible only when these symbols are united to the experiences in our actual, contemporary life which they symbolize . . .⁴⁸

Although Gilkey's terminology is slightly different from that of Gendlin, he is touching on Gendlin's use of experiential meaning, that is, the meaning that comes from being able to symbolize felt, implicitly meaningful experiencing. It is possible, as Gilkey indicates, to speak of the divine in a basically logical or factual way but with little or any <u>experiential meaning</u> in such language for the person. In experiential religion <u>the meaning for the person</u> is primary. Logical and factual religious meanings are neither su-

perfluous nor superseded, but ultimately their importance lies in the ways they can enter into or evoke
"religious experiencing."

While it is true that religions can be approached
analytically, as a kind of conceptual system, or his-
torically, as an homogenous group of revelatory facts,
most religions are initially rooted in at least one
person's lived experience, an experience shared with
and engendered in the hearers or followers.   Often,
however, this experiential understanding of the religion gradually becomes subordinate to non-experiential
elements which are easier to objectify, easier to conceptualize, easier to systematize.   Although perhaps
too stark, Abraham Maslow's criticism of organized
religion is relevant:

> Most people lose or forget the subjec-
> tively religious experience, and define Reli-
> gion as a set of habits, behaviors, dogmas,
> forms, which at the extreme becomes entirely
> legalistic and bureaucratic, conventional,
> empty, and in the truest meaning of the word,
> anti-religious.   The mystic experience, the
> illumination, the great awakening, along with
> the charismatic seer who started the whole
> thing, are forgotten, lost, or transformed
> into their opposites.   Organized religion,
> the churches, finally may become the major
> enemies of the religious experience and the
> religious experiencer.[49]

Even if experiential religion is not completely
lost in the believer, non-experiential religious elements may be experienced in such a way as to produce a
considerable amount of religious confusion.   This confusion can affect "religious experiencing" in three
related ways: "process skipping," "ontologizing," and
"theologizing."

One general way that the process of "religious
experiencing" can be inhibited is through what can be
called "process-skipping."   From some direct experiencing of the divine, a person makes a number of assump-
tions about the divine on the basis of logical or fac-

tual inference, and he or she envisions other characteristics of God, perhaps with the influence of the culture and a given religious tradition. Eventually, the more direct experience of God is not valued enough to be paid attention to. Often, it seems, the person is left with a number of religious concepts and symbols and perhaps a conceptual religious system, but these concepts are no longer a part of his or her "religious experiencing." The concepts are of God, but they are not the person's own concepts of God. In other words, non-experiential religion can easily separate the divine from the person's experiencing process. "Religious experiencing," and the sense of the divine coming from it, is skipped.

Another way the process of "religious experiencing" can be inhibited is by "ontologizing." When the divine (and not the experiencing of the divine) is the focus of religion, it seems that any number of schema is employed to figure out what, or whether, or how this "entity" is, if it is an "entity" at all. Religion becomes a branch of metaphysics, and all the while how God is actually experienced in "living religion" is considered incidental or "merely subjective." "Ontologizing" comes about by forgetting the experiencing subject. Like "process-skipping," it is time-honored and, as James would say, "has the prestige," but its effect can be to stifle "religious experiencing" and, at the same time, to make the focus of religion some kind of "being" cut off from a process from which it might emerge and through which it might unfold.

A third way the process of "religious experiencing" can be inhibited is by "theologizing." As characterized from a perspective of experiential religion, "theologizing" tends to be a highly abstract, critical, and interpretive reflection on the collective experience of a given religious tradition. For the most part, personal religious experience does not, at least explicitly, figure in it. "Experience," as C. Ellis Nelson says, "does not interest theologians very much unless they can generalize it to the human condition or to conceptions of God. These generalizing processes, necessary for theology, remove thought from life."[50] As in "process-skipping" and "ontologizing," "theologizing" can easily move the person away from present felt relating with God with the result that "religious experiencing" becomes at best a secondary concern. As Robert Kinast notes: "By providing a co-herent, intellectual framework, scholarly theology offers greater freedom for experiential reflection but it also runs the risk of separating the fruits of scholarly theology from their experiential roots."[51]

If an understanding of ongoing "religious experiencing" as inherently a process of growth is novel or hard to accept, perhaps some of the difficulty stems from not making a basic distinction between experiential and non-experiential religion. Experiential religion is a process of personal religious growth. Non-experiential religion has no necessary connection with growth, and it tends to side-track "religious experiencing." It may seem to be a simple thing, but it makes a great deal of difference to "living religion" whether one decides to focus consistently on the experiencing of the divine or to focus just on the divine.

b) <u>Experiential religion sees religious symbols, values, and beliefs as interacting with "religious experiencing."</u>

Putting his finger on a central difficulty in presenting the Christian faith, Paul Clifford observes:

> It is not a question, as is still commonly supposed, of translating the faith into language which is more intelligible to ordinary people. The problem is much more complex than that. It is how to relate the Gospel to human feeling, to that all-pervasive substratum of awareness to which I have drawn attention. Until we realize that all attempts to speak to the intellect which do not grapple with underlying feelings will fail, we shall not make any real progress.[52]

An experiential religion insists that religious symbols, beliefs, and values always be understood in relation to someone's experiencing process. The function of these various "contents" would be either to

explicate an individual's concrete, implicitly meaningful "religious experiencing" or to evoke or engender
"religious experiencing," much as Rudolf Otto suggests
in The Idea of the Holy.[53]   In either case, symbols,
beliefs, and values will not be seen as having a life
of their own apart from an actual experiencing process.

     Not to see these religious "contents" as aspects
of "religious experiencing" would be to suffer, in
Whitehead's phrase, "the fallacy of misplaced concreteness." The reality is not in the religious concepts
and beliefs, as James has shown, but in the more primary religious feeling which underlies them. The function of these "contents," that is, the concepts and
beliefs, is precisely to symbolize this more primary
experiencing, to capture it, to complete it, and to
carry it forward as a process.

     In experiential religion the focus is on bodily-
felt-relating to the divine, an organism-environment
process. To emphasize symbols at the expense of this
process is to distort the reality of primary experiencing or to make light of felt meaning, which is the
only basis on which the symbols themselves can function
experientially and can aid in ongoing growth and development. Gendlin is himself insistent on the tie
between religion and felt meaning as well as on the
dependent role of conceptualization when he states:

          Religious services, strong emotions, our
     acquaintance with persons--these are all
     cases where meaning certainly is experienced,
     but because our verbal symbols usually are
     inadequate, we are aware strongly of felt
     meaning. At least some of this meaning usu-
     ally can be explicated in terms of verbal
     symbols. Whether so explicated or not, felt
     meaning is experienced in these cases and we
     may easily demonstrate its presence to our-
     selves.[54]

     The fact that "religious experiencing" is the mat-
rix for the different "contents" of religion is especially significant for an understanding of religious
values and beliefs. As Gendlin points out, it is not

the values as conceptualized which are important but the valuing process out of which such values come. This insight is crucial for experiential religion. It is crucial because it means "religious experiencing" is also a process of religious valuing. In addition, it is crucial because it shows that to identify religion simply as a collection of "value-conclusions" is again to submerge experiencing in a way that can leave religious values static, unowned, and merely formal. A religious "value-conclusion" (for example, "God is love"), can be the symbolization of a religious valuing process, or at least compatible with it, but it can also be adopted as if it were compatible with experiencing when it is not. To the extent the latter is the case, the person loses touch with "religious experiencing;" his or her religion is no longer experiential; the process of religious growth is blocked.

What is true of religious values seems equally true of religious beliefs. For experiential religion, importance lies not in the "contents" of belief but in the felt process of meaning these contents are meant to convey. The <u>believing process</u> of the person has primacy, not the verbal formulations.

. . . believing is not commanded by beliefs. Beliefs come from believing; and believing is generated in experience. Believing finds satisfaction only in such statements as both <u>express</u> <u>and</u> <u>enhance</u> the whole scope and intensity of the experience from which it arises and to which it must contribute.[55]

Experiential religion understands the person as a valuing and believing process. The symbols or concepts are significant to the extent that they can explicate or engender this process as it presently is, and thereby carry it forward. As Gendlin says:

There is no way to do without the concrete experiencing. Psychological, religious, or other concepts cannot purport to be the conceptual structure of experiencing. In each discourse we must ask, instead, what aspects

116

of experiencing these or those concepts help
us differentiate and refer to.[56]

c) Experiential religion is engendered by interpersonal
   experiencing and is a manner of experiencing.

   The previous section, "Religious Experiencing and
Growth," set forth the role of the interpersonal
"other" in engendering religious experiencing and
growth. A listener who was open to "religious experiencing" provided a context in which the woman who
felt "something in the way" in her relating to God was
able to focus on that felt relating and allow it to
become more ongoing. Similarly, James Clark, a sensitivity trainer with an understanding of religion as
process, showed that "religious experiencing" can be
evoked and deepened in members of the group. Experiential religion is engendered or furthered by a process
of interpersonal experiencing.

   When James defines religion as the feelings, acts,
and experiences of individuals "in their solitude,"[57]
he seemed to exclude the interpersonal aspect of religious experience. Gendlin's thinking brings greater
clarity to "religious experiencing" by allowing one to
see that, while the locus of religion is in the person,
the process is always, to a greater or lesser extent, a
function of interpersonal experiencing.

   In the broadest sense, the religious symbols a
person may use are in some way derivative of the culture, the traditions, and the communities in which he
or she lives. An experiential religion points to the
fact that no experiencing is in a vacuum. In a more
immediate sense, the specific symbols a person uses to
explicate present feeling in relation to the divine are
often dependent on an other who can help facilitate
that process. Most significant for experiential religion, however, is the fact that one person's openness
to "religious experiencing" seems able to engender
the process of "religious experiencing" in another.

   In the context of a group, an inter-engendering of
"religious experiencing" can occur. As James Clark
finds, there is something in the interpersonal expe-

117

riencing of the group that fosters the kind of experiencing in its members which calls for religious symbolization. Corroborating Clark's findings, Joseph
Havens observes that "important religious feelings and
experiences can occur within and be engendered by group
encounter."[58] Like Clark, Havens suggests that this
phenomenon is at least partly attributable to the group
leader whose "legitimate function is to be aware of the
transcendental possibilities, to trust the group's
ability to move toward them, and, occasionally, to
point out the wider referent or meaning of a particular
group experience."[59]

With the focus on "religious experiencing" in an
interpersonal setting, it is easy to see that the
experiencing engendered is often felt as more alive,
energized, and open. Clark refers to this changed manner of experiencing when he points out "people can,
under appropriate conditions, experience the exhilara-
tion of discovering and expressing their own love and
power with one another."[60] The interpersonal encounter
brings about a new manner of experiencing, and it is
really out of this new manner of experiencing that
religious symbolization seems to come. In other words,
there is a connection between the manner of experiencing as generated interpersonally and "religious experiencing." This connection suggests that in experiential religion what transpires is the interaction of one
process of "religious experiencing" with another, an
interaction that is not primarily concept to concept,
but process to process, and especially felt-aliveness
to felt-aliveness. Non-experiential religion may be
transmitted conceptually. Experiential religion is
engendered or evoked when the symbols transmitted come
from the sharing of "religious experiencing."

4. Implications of Religious Experiencing for Religious Education, Pastoral Counseling, and Spiritual Direction

Since "religious experiencing" is an "ur-
phenomenon" which is inherently a process of growth and
from which an understanding of experiential religion
clearly flows, there is a number of implications of
this phenomenon for various religious activities. Tak-

ing a practical focus, this final section of the chapter considers briefly some of the implications of "religious experiencing" for religious education, pastoral counseling, and spiritual direction. Although not considered here, there are other implications of "religious experiencing" that help to recapture and redefine constitutive elements of theology and spirituality.[61] In addition, a number of religious themes such as prayer, the will of God, conscience, vocation, discernment, meditation, and mysticism can also be articulated from its perspective.

a) Religious Education

Much of the contemporary approach to religious education is in a "schooling-instructional paradigm"[62] in which the transmission of "value-conclusions" and "belief-conclusions" is the central concern. As Gabriel Moran characterizes this approach:

It is assumed that there is a body of materials that is the content of Christian faith, and that the teacher's role is to convince people to accept this content as true. These days the content consists of a large, technical collection of exegetical, historical, and theological materials.[63]

In light of the description of experiential religion, it is possible to envision a shift of focus in religious education from the handing on of "contents" to a primary concern for each person's experiencing of God. James Michael Lee reflects the goal of this shift when he says:

The fundamental operative pedagogical principle which should guide the religious educator is that of structuring the pedagogical variables in such a way that the learner comes to an experience of or with God as the divine presents himself in one or another of his manifestations.[64]

The notion of "religious experiencing" consolidates and specifies this shift in a very concrete and practical way. Not only is the primary focus no longer on the verbal content but rather on the person and "experience of or with God," but also now both these latter elements are in the one phenomenon of "religious experiencing." Moreover, this "religious experiencing," when directly referred to and engendered, reveals itself as a process of religious growth--a major concern of religious education. "After all," as Lee states, "the primary goal of religious instruction is immediate concrete experienced religious living," and not verbal abstractions which ultimately are drawn from "immediate concrete experienced religious living."[65]

Simply put, this shift in approach to religious education is from the primacy of the conceptual to the primacy of experiencing. The "content" of the faith, that is, the beliefs and values of the tradition, is still essential to religious education, but now it is understood much more in terms of the explicit meaning surfacing from the shared "religious experiencing" of the group. The role of religious concepts is "not so much to give knowledge as to evoke a religious experience in the hearer similar to the one had by the person formulating the symbol."[66] The shift is from "knowledge about" to "knowledge of acquaintance," from a factual to an experiential use of concepts, from a distanced phenomenology of religious experience to one that is more immediate.

Stressing the primacy of religious experiencing, James Michael Lee observes:

> Religious language arises from religious experience and/or points to religious experience and/or describes religious experience and/or seeks to clarify and interpret religious experience. The past, present, and future primacy must therefore rest ultimately on religious experience, not on religious language. The religious educator never ought to allow religious language to get in the way of religious experience.[67]

John Westerhoff describes a similar primacy of religious experiencing over the conceptual in the context of the religious community:

> For faith, it is therefore especially
> important to acknowledge that the most sig-
> nificant and fundamental form of learning is
> experience. Later a person may "image" that
> experience, and even later conceptualize it.
> But we begin by experiencing life in a commu-
> nity which seeks the good of others, then we
> learn the story of the Good Samaritan, and
> finally through reflection on an experience
> ("doing theology") we symbolically conceptu-
> alize the community of God in terms of love,
> justice, and equity. Each of these steps in
> learning occurs in order, and each is essen-
> tial to the following step. But at the
> beginning is experience.[68]

From a clearly developmental perspective, Ana-
Maria Rizzuto's research shows rather convincingly that
it is out of the young child's experience of the primal
community of parents and significant others that the
image of God is basically formed. As Rizzuto puts it:
"No child arrives at 'the house of God' without his pet
God under his arm."[69] During the school years, as the
child learns the traditions of the community and the
culture, the child may experience various images of the
"God of the Community" and the "God of the Culture,"
but for the most part these images remain a nuancing
and an amplifying of the earlier "religious experiencing" expressed in the "pet God."

As the young person comes to adulthood, what seems
to be crucial as a foundation for mature faith is that
all these images of God become transformed and inte-
grated as part of the person's own experience of God.
At this point, being able to focus on "religious experiencing," especially in the context of the shared
"religious experiencing" of a faith group, will be most
helpful, if not essential, for continuing religious
growth.

All along the way to personal religious faith,
however, if "process-skipping" is to be avoided and if
religious education is to be personally meaningful,

121

"religious experiencing" needs to be addressed, at times by focusing, at times by engendering in a small group, at times, perhaps, by a host of other less direct ways. If growth in relating to God is a primary concern of religious education, then paying attention to each person's "religious experiencing" is clearly focal in the facilitation of this growth.

b) Pastoral Counseling

It is safe to say that in the field of pastoral counseling there is as little consensus as there is in religious education. There are as many definitions of pastoral counseling as there are pastoral counselors. What makes a definition so difficult is that there is any number of ways of saying who a "pastor" is. There is any number of understandings of "ministry" and "church." There is any number of ways to describe who a "person" is and what "problems" are. And there is any number of theories describing "counseling" or "psychotherapy" and what it is intended to bring about.

Keeping in mind the tenuousness and incompleteness of any definition of pastoral counseling, two fairly representative definitions help to situate this religious activity in relation to "religious experiencing." Edward Thornton sees pastoral counseling as "a form of religious ministry which integrates the findings of behavioral science and theology in the effort to prepare the way for divine-human encounter in the midst of human crises."[70] William Hulme defines it as "a ministry to persons, couples, and families that assists them in working through pressing problems in their relationship to themselves, to others, and to God."[71] In both these definitions the person's relationship with God is constitutive, and in both definitions there is at least the implication that this relationship is bound up with other problems of a person's life. If these elements of a definition are viewed from an experiential perspective, then pastoral counseling has as a primary concern any blocks in a person's living and experiencing, especially as these are part of blocked "religious experiencing."

Within the past century a split has developed

between "theology" and a newer "behavioral science."
These concepts have come to stand for different academic fields, often with distinctly different methodol-
ogies and subject matter. If not born of this split,
pastoral counseling has been raised in it and has had
to respond to it in one way or another. James Ewing
observes:

> Pastoral counseling is rooted in two dis-
> ciplines of knowledge: religion and behav-
> ioral science. While both fields have an
> identifiable integrity, the interplay between
> them is difficult to resolve both methodolog-
> ically and conceptually.[72]

Because "religious experiencing" is at once a
religious and a psychological phenomenon, it is a
"place to look" for an integration of these two disciplines. Because it is such a basic living phenomenon,
it is a "place to stand" which is "no place at all."
"Religious experiencing" is prior to the abstractive
academic, methodological "stands" which seek to elaborate and interpret it.[73]

As C. Ellis Nelson makes clear:

> Theology and psychology are subjects: that
> is, fields of thought that have a history and
> literature. It is easy to study these sub-
> jects and forget that both are dealing with
> human beings and that somehow both have to be
> reconciled within personal experience.[74]

"Religious experiencing" as a dimension of the
over-all experiencing of the person is just such a
place of reconciliation within personal experience.
This is true not only in principle but also in reality
as the person's problems are actually addressed and
change occurs in the process of pastoral counseling.
James Ewing touches this kind of reconciliation when he
points out:

> What we know of psychological personality
> structure and religious symbols allows us to
> understand the conflict or stress a person is

123

suffering. If the conflict is resolved through the pastor-therapist's intervention, then change takes place both in the development of healthier personality and of more adequate "God-symbols" (i.e., ideas, and expressions for relating to God) that allow internal meaning and direction to shift. Psychological structures and religious symbols intertwine so that one intimately affects the other.[75]

In experiential terms, if the pastoral counselor helps the client pay attention to stopped or blocked experiencing in other areas of his or her life, a changed manner of "religious experiencing" may also occur. Conversely, if the pastoral counselor helps the client to focus directly on blocked "religious experiencing," then the change which may occur in the felt relating to the divine will often have "global application" to other areas of experiencing as well.

The most direct implication of "religious experiencing" for pastoral counseling is for blocked or frozen relating to the divine. In the section above on "Religious Experiencing and Growth" a number of general scenarios were sketched to show how this blocked relating to God occurs.[76] An understanding of "religious experiencing" suggests that in a given person the manner of felt relating to God can be described on a kind of continuum, from "frozen," "distanced," "non-process" at the one end moving to "very immediate," "flowing," and "unfolding" at the other. A primary concern of pastoral counseling is, when appropriate, to help the client's felt sense of relating to God to move along this continuum.

Finally, if growth in "religious experiencing" includes a shared process of one person's felt relating to the divine with that of another, then it seems essential that the pastoral counselor be comfortable with his or her own process of "religious experiencing" and be welcoming of this dimension in the experiencing of the client.

c) Spiritual Direction

We do not need elaborate techniques. We do not have to be "holy" in some other-worldly sense. We do need some biblical and theological knowledge. But most of all, we need an interest in and a willingness to explore religious experience with those who seek us out, uncovering together the relationship which this experience is revealing.[77]

If exploring religious experience is of the essence of spiritual guidance or direction, and if as Barry and Connolly, the authors of The Practice of Spiritual Direction, suggest, "religious experience is to spiritual direction what foodstuff is to cooking,"[78] then helping a person to focus consistently on "religious experiencing" is a helpful way to bring about the kind of religious process spiritual directors seek to engender and support.

Spiritual direction offers a person the opportunity to become more aware of his or her experience of God. While this awareness is also a major concern in pastoral counseling, there the focus is usually on blocked or structure-bound "religious experiencing," that is, on those things that are in the way of relating to the divine. In spiritual direction, on the other hand, the focus is on a basically alive and ongoing relationship with God. What blocks are there are for the most part in the relationship itself, as, for example, in the transcript in the section on "Religious Experiencing and Growth" of the woman who felt "something in the way" in her relating to God. The goal of spiritual direction is to allow "religious experiencing" to deepen and unfold toward saintliness and union with God.

Focusing on "religious experiencing" in spiritual direction seems to have a twofold thrust. It allows the person to know organismically just how he or she is in relating to God, to articulate the sense of this in just those words or images which capture it, and perhaps to experience a felt shift of further movement in the relationship. At the same time, by letting the person experience just how he or she presently is with God, focusing on "religious experiencing" provides an excellent starting point for prayer and may, in fact, be experienced as prayer itself. Prayer is the experiencing of a living relationship with God, and as such, it is implicit in the way the purpose of spiritual direction is defined. William Barry, for example, finds that the purpose of direction is "to help another to relate consciously to the living God and to let God relate to him, to grow in that relationship, and to live in its truth"[79]

One of the primary concerns of spiritual direction is to allow the directee to grow in a way that is respectful of his or her unique relationship with God.

> The only valid objective of spiritual direction is growth of the directee. What growth consists in for the person in question is not to be determined by the guide, much less by a third party. It must be worked out by the directee in his/her relationship with God. The spiritual guide is at the service of the directee's own spiritual project, not of someone else's (or the director's own!) project for the person.[80]

Assisting a person to stay with "religious experiencing" is one clear way to let the unique sense of direction in the relationship with the divine come from within. The process is dictated to neither by the spiritual director nor by the "value-conclusions" of the tradition nor even by the directee himself or herself. Often what comes through focusing on "religious experiencing" is quite different from what either the focuser or the guide expected to find.

At times, a person will seek out spiritual guidance in order to discover the will of God and a future direction in life. A crisis or a call to "something more" may be experienced, but it is often not at all clear what this is about. If the goal is to enable the person to find the will of God uniquely for her or him, then the spiritual guide's role is to facilitate the directee's actual experiencing of God and not to do anything that would draw away from this vital process. As Gendlin makes clear:

> In therapy, one person cannot guide another. It succeeds only if both people know that the criterion of therapy at every juncture is the "patient's" <u>inwardly arising</u> steps. It is odd that we would willingly surrender that process for any purpose, but especially when the purpose is that very process! And yet, in psychotherapeutic and spiritual matters we are most prone to do so. Since we seek a change in ourselves, of course we must mistrust our own judgment. But to go by another person's judgment gives up on just that inward development which is the purpose of the activity.
>
> In spiritual concerns, par excellence, this contradiction must be seen. We do need others to relate to, and we need them to help us, but help with what? With an inwardly arising process. How can we be helped, if we try to give that up from the start?[81]

ENDNOTES

1   Ralph Barton Perry, <u>The Thought and Character of William James</u>, (Briefer Version) New York, Harper Torchbooks, 1964, p. 259.

2   William James, <u>The Varieties of Religious Experience</u>, Cambridge, Harvard University Press, 1985, p. 395.

3   <u>Ibid.</u>, p. 341.

4   <u>Ibid.</u>, p. 340.

5 Eugene T. Gendlin, <u>Experiencing</u> <u>and</u> <u>the</u> <u>Creation</u> <u>of</u> <u>Meaning</u>, New York, Free Press of Glencoe, 1962, p. 46.

6 James, <u>The</u> <u>Varieties</u> <u>of</u> <u>Religious</u> <u>Experience</u>, p. 75.

7 William James, <u>The</u> <u>Principles</u> <u>of</u> <u>Psychology</u>, Vol. 1, Cambridge, Harvard University Press, 1981, p. 218.

8 The point being made is that James does not <u>consistently</u> see feeling as something bodily felt. In speaking of how James understands the "self," Robert R. Ehman, "William James and the Structure of the Self," <u>New</u> <u>Essays</u> <u>in</u> <u>Phenomenology</u>: <u>Studies</u> <u>in</u> <u>the</u> <u>Philosophy</u> <u>of</u> <u>Experience</u>, James M. Edie, ed., Chicago, Quadrangle, 1969, p. 258, observes: "He is not concerned with the self or with conscious life primarily as a measurable and objectifiable entity; and he does not take the measured locomotion of physical objects in space as the model for the understanding of the flow of conscious life. More basic than its measurable and objective character is its flowing, streaming, <u>felt</u> <u>bodily</u> <u>life</u>." (Emphasis mine)

9 James, <u>The</u> <u>Varieties</u> <u>of</u> <u>Religious</u> <u>Experience</u>, p. 39.

10 <u>Ibid</u>., p. 40.

11 <u>Ibid</u>., p. 59.

12 <u>Ibid</u>., p. 36.

13 <u>Ibid</u>., p. 31.

14 <u>Ibid</u>., p. 66.

15 <u>Ibid</u>., p. 395.

16 <u>Ibid</u>., p. 67.

17 <u>Ibid</u>., p. 96.

18 James, The Principles of Psychology, Vol. 1, p. 175.

19 Ibid., p. 190, note 8.

20 See Walter Smet, S.J., "Religious Experience in Client-Centered Therapy," The Human Person, Magda B. Arnold and John A. Casson, S.J., eds., New York, Ronald Press, 1954, p. 540-542.

21 James, The Varieties of Religious Experience, p. 163.

22 Ibid., p. 95.

23 Ibid., p. 173.

24 James, The Principles of Psychology, Vol. 1, p. 246.

25 Ibid., p. 442.

26 William James, Some Problems of Philosophy, Cambridge, Harvard University Press, 1979, p. 34.

27 James, The Varieties of Religious Experience, p. 219-221.

28 See, for example, Rodney Stark, "A Taxonomy of Religious Experience," Journal for the Scientific Study of Religion, Vol. 5, No. 1, October 1965, p. 97-116.

29 I am thinking here both of a sense of sin as an "obstacle" in relating to God and of an understanding of God in terms of demands that do not seem realizable.

30 One of the things I am thinking of here is the child's experience of the "Superego God," an accusatory authority, a divine guarantor of guilt. Developmentally, this God of Guilt can be seen as established at Erikson's Stage 3, Initiative versus Guilt. At the time when identity can be realized, that is, as late adolescence moves into

young adulthood, perhaps this "Superego God" can be begun to be transcended in a "God of Personal Experience." For a very helpful description of the "Superego God" see Peter Homans, "Toward a Psychology of Religion: By Way of Freud and Tillich," The Dialogue Between Theology and Psychology, Peter Homans, ed., Chicago, University of Chicago Press, 1968, p. 53-81. For the relation of personal identity to faith see Leland Elhard, "Living Faith: Some Contributions of the Concept of Ego-identity to the Understanding of Faith," ibid, p. 135-161.

31 I am thinking here of anthropomorphism, which, along with rationalism and authoritarianism, is seen as one of three "stumbling blocks" that help to keep religious feeling repressed according to Viktor Frankl, The Will To Meaning, New York, New American Library, 1969, p. 149. From a Piagetian perspective on cognitive religious development, Ronald Goldman, Religious Thinking From Childhood to Adolescence, New York, Seabury, 1968, p. 227, observes: "it is of interest to see that anthropomorphic concepts tend to continue until about the time when propositional thinking begins and concrete operational thinking is on the decline. We are forced to the conclusion that religious concepts introduced too soon may lead to regressive thinking in religion, and not only retard later insights but may prevent them developing at all."

32 This session is recounted with permission.

33 James J. Tracy, "Faith and Growth: A Psychology of Faith," Insight, Vol. 5, No. 3, Winter 1967, p. 16.

34 Orlo Strunk, Jr., Mature Religion: A Psychological Study, New York, Abingdon, 1965, p. 125.

35 James, The Varieties of Religious Experience, p. 146.

36 Ibid., p. 220.

37   James V. Clark, "Toward a Theory and Practice of Religious Experiencing," <u>Challenges of Humanistic Psychology</u>, James F. T. Bugental, ed., New York, McGraw-Hill, 1967, p. 253.

38   <u>Ibid</u>., p. 255.

39   <u>Ibid</u>., p. 255-256.

40   <u>Ibid</u>., p. 254.

41   <u>Ibid</u>., p. 256-257. (The quote is from Martin Buber, <u>The Knowledge of Man</u>, New York, Harper Torchbooks, 1965, p. 71.)

42   <u>Ibid</u>., p. 257.

43   Paul Rowntree Clifford, "The Place of Feeling in Religious Awareness," <u>New Theology No. 7: The Recovery of Transcendence</u>, Martin E. Marty and Dean G. Peerman, eds., Macmillan, 1970, p. 52.

44   Kilian McDonnell, O.S.B., "I Believe That I Might Experience," <u>Theological Field Education: A Collection of Key Resources</u>, Donald F. Beisswenger, Tjaard G. Hommes, and Doran McCarty, eds., The Association for Theological Field Education, 1981, p. 80.

45   <u>Ibid</u>., p. 80-81.

46   <u>Ibid</u>., p. 81.

47   Morton Kelsey, <u>Encounter With God: A Theology of Christian Experience</u>, Minneapolis, Bethany Fellowship, 1972, p. 24-25.

48   Langdon Gilkey, "The Problem of God: A Programmatic Essay," <u>Traces of God in a Secular Culture</u>, George F. McLean, O.M.I., ed., New York, Alba House, 1973, p. 18.

49   Abraham H. Maslow, <u>Religions, Values, and Peak-Experiences</u>, New York, Viking Press, 1970, p. viii.

50 C. Ellis Nelson, "Theological Foundations for Religious Education," Changing Patterns of Religious Education, Marvin J. Taylor, ed., Nashville, Abingdon, 1984, p. 12.

51 Robert L. Kinast, "Orthopraxis: Starting Point for Theology," Proceedings of the Catholic Theological Society of America, Vol. 38., 1983, p. 33.

52 Clifford, "The Place of Feeling in Religious Awareness," p. 52.

53 Rudolf Otto, The Idea of the Holy, John W. Harvey, trans., New York, Oxford University Press, 1958, p. 6.

54 Gendlin, Experiencing and the Creation of Meaning, p. 70-71.

55 Richard R. Niebuhr, Experiential Religion, New York, Harper & Row, 1972, p. 69.

56 Eugene T. Gendlin, "Experiencing and the Nature of Concepts," The Christian Scholar, Vol. 46, No. 2, Fall 1963, p. 253-254.

57 James, The Varieties of Religious Experience, p. 34.

58 Joseph Havens, "Religious Awareness and Small Groups: Warmth versus Enlightenment," The Dialogue Between Theology and Psychology, Peter Homans, ed., Chicago, University of Chicago Press, 1968, p. 264.

59 Ibid., p. 280.

60 Clark, "Toward a Theory and Practice of Religious Experiencing," p. 254.

61 For a very helpful understanding of spirituality in light of Gendlin's thinking see Peter A. Campbell and Edwin M. McMahon, Bio-Spirituality: Focusing as a Way to Grow, Chicago, Loyola University Press, 1985.

62 John H. Westerhoff III, _Will Our Children Have Faith?_ New York, Seabury Press, 1983, p. 6.

63 Gabriel Moran, F.S.C., _Vision and Tactics: Toward an Adult Church_, New York, Herder and Herder, 1968, p. 63.

64 James Michael Lee, _The Content of Religious Instruction: A Social Science Approach_, Birmingham, Religious Education Press, 1985, p. 63-64.

65 _Ibid._, p. 116.

66 Seely Beggiani, "Revelation and Religious Experience," _New Dimensions in Religious Experience_, George Devine, ed., New York, Alba House, 1971, p. 46-47.

67 Lee, _The Content of Religious Instruction_ p. 285.

68 Westerhoff, _Will Our Children Have Faith?_ p. 63-64.

69 Ana-Maria Rizzuto, _The Birth of the Living God: A Psychoanalytic Study_, Chicago, University of Chicago Press, 1979, p. 8.

70 Edward E. Thornton, _Theology and Pastoral Counseling_, Englewood Cliffs, New Jersey, Prentice-Hall, 1964, p. 27.

71 William E. Hulme, _Pastoral Care and Counseling: Using the Unique Resources of the Christian Tradition_, Minneapolis, Augsburg, 1981, p. 9.

72 James W. Ewing, "Epilogue: Pastoral Counseling Issues: Current and Future," _Pastoral Counseling_, Barry K. Estadt, Melvin Blanchette, John R. Compton, eds., Englewood Cliffs, New Jersey, 1983, p. 287.

73 Paul Tillich, _Systematic Theology_, Vol. 1, New York, Harper & Row, 1967, p. 26.

74 C. Ellis Nelson, ed., _Conscience: Theological and Psychological Perspectives_, New York, Newman, 1973, p. 167.

75 James W. Ewing, "The Pastoral Therapeutic Stance," _Psychiatry, Ministry and Pastoral Counseling_, A. W. Richard Sipe and Clarence J. Rowe, eds., Collegeville, Minnesota, Liturgical Press, 1984, p. 66.

76 See above, p. 99.

77 William A. Barry and William J. Connolly, _The Practice of Spiritual Direction_, New York, Seabury Press, 1982, p. 20.

78 _Ibid._, p. 8.

79 William Barry, S.J., "Prayer in Pastoral Care: A Contribution from the Tradition of Spiritual Direction," _Spiritual Direction: Contemporary Readings_, Kevin G. Culligan, O.C.D., ed., Locust Valley, New York, Living Flame Press, 1983, p. 72.

80 Sandra M. Schneiders, I.H.M., "The Contemporary Ministry of Spiritual Direction," _Chicago Studies_, Vol. 15, Spring 1976, p. 126.

81 Eugene T. Gendlin, "The Obedience Pattern," _Studies in Formative Spirituality_, Vol. 5, No. 2, May 1984, p. 191.

BIBLIOGRAPHY

Allport, Gordon W., The Use of Personal Documents in Psychological Science, New York, Social Science Research Council, 1942.

Ayer, A. J., The Origins of Pragmatism: Studies in the Philosophy of Charles Sanders Peirce and William James, London, Macmillan, 1968.

Barry, William, S.J., "Prayer in Pastoral Care: A Contribution from the Tradition of Spiritual Direction," Spiritual Direction: Contemporary Readings, Kevin G. Culligan, O.C.D., ed., Locust Valley, New York, Living Flame Press, 1983, p. 72-79

Barry, William A., and William J. Connolly, The Practice of Spiritual Direction, New York, Seabury Press, 1982.

Beggiani, Seely, "Revelation and Religious Experience," New Dimensions in Religious Experience, George Devine, ed., New York, Alba House, 1971, p. 39-51.

Boodin, John Elof, "William James as I Knew Him, II," The Personalist, Vol. 23, No. 2, Summer 1942, p. 279-290.

Bowers, Fredson, prep., "The Text of The Varieties of Religious Experience," The Varieties of Religious Experience, Cambridge, Harvard University Press, 1985, p. 520-587.

Bozzo, Edward George, "James and the Valence of Human Action," Journal of Religion and Health, Vol. 16, No. 1, January 1977, p. 26-43.

Brown, James F., Affectivity: Its Language and Meaning, Washington, University Press of America, 1982.

Buber, Martin, The Knowledge of Man, New York, Harper Torchbooks, 1965.

Campbell Peter A., and Edwin M. McMahon, Bio-Spirituality: Focusing as a Way to Grow, Chicago, Loyola University Press, 1985.

Clark, James V., "Toward a Theory and Practice of Religious Experiencing," Challenges of Humanistic Psychology, James F. T. Bugental, ed., New York, McGraw-Hill, 1967, p. 253-258.

Clifford, Paul Rowntree, "The Place of Feeling in Religious Awareness," New Theology No. 7: The Recovery of Transcendence, Martin E. Marty and Dean G. Peerman, eds., Macmillan, 1970, p. 47-55.

Dewey, John, Experience and Nature, Second Edition, New York, Dover, 1958.

Edie, James M., "William James and The Phenomenology of Religious Experience," American Philosophy and the Future: Essays for a New Generation, Michael Novak, ed., New York, Scribner's, 1968, p. 247-269.

Ehman, Robert R., "William James and the Structure of the Self," New Essays in Phenomenology: Studies in the Philosophy of Experience, James M. Edie, ed., Chicago, Quadrangle, 1969, p. 256-270.

Elhard, Leland, "Living Faith: Some Contributions of the Concept of Ego-identity to the Understanding of Faith," The Dialogue Between Theology and Psychology, Peter Homans, ed., Chicago, University of Chicago Press, 1968. p. 135-161.

Ewing, James W., "Epilogue: Pastoral Counseling Issues: Current and Future," Pastoral Counseling, Barry K. Estadt, Melvin Blanchette, John R. Compton, eds., Englewood Cliffs, New Jersey, 1983, p. 287-296.

_____, "The Pastoral Therapeutic Stance," Psychiatry, Ministry and Pastoral Counseling, A. W. Richard Sipe and Clarence J. Rowe, eds., Collegeville, Minnesota, Liturgical Press, 1984, p. 64-77.

Frankl, Viktor, The Will To Meaning, New York, New American Library, 1969.

Gendlin, Eugene T., "Analysis," Martin Heidegger, _What Is a Thing?_ W. B. Barton, Jr., and Vera Deutsch, trans., Chicago, Regnery, 1967, p. 247-296.

_____, "The Discovery of Felt Meaning," _Language and Meaning_, James B. Macdonald and Robert R. Leeper, eds., Washington, D.C., National Education Association, 1966, p. 45-62.

_____, "Existentialism and Experiential Psychotherapy," _Existential Child Therapy: The Child's Discovery of Himself_, Clark Moustakas, ed., New York, Basic Books, 1966, p. 206-246.

_____, "Experiencing: A Variable in the Process of Therapeutic Change," _The American Journal of Psychotherapy_, Vol. 15, No. 2, April 1961, p. 233-245.

_____, _Experiencing and the Creation of Meaning: a Philosophical and Psychological Approach to the Subjective_, New York, Free Press of Glencoe, 1962.

_____, "Experiencing and the Nature of Concepts," _The Christian Scholar_, Vol. 46, No. 3, Fall 1963, p. 245-255.

_____, "Experiential Explication and Truth," _Journal of Existentialism_, Vol. 6, No. 22, Winter 1965-66, p. 131-146.

_____, "Experiential Phenomenology," _Phenomenology and the Social Sciences_, Vol. 1, Maurice Natanson, ed., Evanston, Illinois, Northwestern University Press, 1973, p. 281-319.

_____, "Experiential Psychotherapy," _Current Psychotherapies_, Raymond Corsini, ed., Itasca, Illinois, Peacock, 1973, p. 317-352.

_____, "Experiential Psychotherapy," _Current Psychotherapies_, Second Edition, Raymond Corsini, ed., Itasca, Illinois, Peacock, 1979, p. 340-373.

_____, _Experiential Psychotherapy_, manuscript for publication, no date.

_____, Focusing, New York, Bantam, 1981.

_____, Focusing, New York, Everest House, 1978.

_____, "Focusing," Psychotherapy: Theory, Research and Practice, Vol. 6, No. 1, Winter 1969, p. 4-15.

_____, "A Focusing Intensive Workshop," (four audio tapes), The Focusing Institute and Terra Nova Films, Inc., 1983.

_____, "How I Teach Focusing--1979," mimeographed, p. 1-16.

_____, Let Your Body Interpret Your Dreams, Wilmette, Illinois, Chiron Publications, 1986.

_____, "Neurosis and Human Nature in the Experiential Method of Thought and Therapy," Humanitas, Vol. 3, No. 2, Fall 1967, p. 139-152.

_____, "The Obedience Pattern," Studies in Formative Spirituality, Vol. 5, No. 2, May 1984, p. 189-202.

_____, "The Role of Knowledge in Practice," The Counselor's Handbook, Gail F. Farwell, Neal R. Gamsky and Philippa Mathieu-Coughlan, eds., New York, Intext Educational Publishers, 1974, p. 269-294.

_____, "A Theory of Personality Change," New Directions in Client-Centered Therapy, J. T. Hart and T. M. Tomlinson, eds., Boston, Houghton Mifflin, 1970, p. 129-173.

_____, "Values and the Process of Experiencing," The Goals of Psychotherapy, Alvin R. Mahrer, ed., New York, Appleton-Century-Crofts, 1967, p. 180-205.

Gendlin, Eugene T., John Beebe III, James Cassens, Marjorie Klein, and Mark Oberlander, "Focusing Ability in Psychotherapy, Personality, and Creativity," Research in Psychotherapy, Vol. 3, John M. Shlien, ed., Washington, D.C., American Psychological Association,

1967, p. 217-238.

Gilkey, Langdon, "The Problem of God: A Programmatic Essay," Traces of God in a Secular Culture, George F. McLean, O.M.I., ed., New York, Alba House, 1973, p. 3-23.

Gilmore, Ronald M., "William James and Religious Language: Daughters of Earth, Sons of Heaven?" Eglise et Theologie, Vol. 4, No. 3, 1973, p. 359-390.

Gobar, Ash, "The Phenomenology of William James," Proceedings of The American Philosophical Society, Vol. 114, No. 4, August 1970, p. 294-309.

Goldman, Ronald, Religious Thinking From Childhood to Adolescence, New York, Seabury, 1968.

Havens, Joseph, "Religious Awareness and Small Groups: Warmth versus Enlightenment," The Dialogue Between Theology and Psychology, Peter Homans, ed., Chicago, University of Chicago Press, 1968, p. 263-284.

Hay, David, "Re-Review: William James' The Varieties of Religious Experience," The Modern Churchman, N.S., XXVII, No. 2, 1985, p. 45-49.

Heard, Gerald, "Can This Drug Enlarge Man's Mind?" The Psychedelic Reader, Gunther M. Weil, Ralph Metzner, and Timothy Leary, eds., New York, Citadel, 1971, p. 7-13.

Homans, Peter, "Toward a Psychology of Religion: By Way of Freud and Tillich," The Dialogue Between Theology and Psychology, Peter Homans, ed., Chicago, University of Chicago Press, 1968, p. 53-81.

Hulme, William E., Pastoral Care and Counseling: Using the Unique Resources of the Christian Tradition, Minneapolis, Augsburg, 1981.

James, Henry, ed., The Letters of William James, Vol. II, Boston, Atlantic Monthly Press, 1920.

James, William, "Another non-religious type," in

"J. Memoranda for Gifford Lectures. Original Plan for a philosophical second volume. 1900 plus," Notebooks, MS Box L, James Archives, Houghton Library, Harvard University, Cambridge.

_____, "Diary 1868," MS Box L, James Archives, Houghton Library, Harvard University, Cambridge.

_____, _Essays in Radical Empiricism_, Cambridge, Harvard University Press, 1976.

_____, "'Experience,' from Baldwin's _Dictionary_," _Essays in Philosophy_, Cambridge, Harvard University Press, 1978, p. 95.

_____, ed., "Introduction," _The Literary Remains of the Late Henry James_, Boston, Osgood, 1885, p. 7-119.

_____, "On Some Hegelisms," _Mind_, Vol. 7, No. 26, April 1882, p. 186-208.

_____, _A Pluralistic Universe_, Cambridge, Harvard University Press, 1977.

_____, _Pragmatism_, Cambridge, Harvard University Press, 1978.

_____, _The Principles of Psychology_, Vol. I, Cambridge, Harvard University Press, 1981.

_____, Review of Benjamin Paul Blood, _Anaesthetic Revelation_, _Atlantic Monthly_, Vol. 34, 1874, p. 627-629.

_____, _Some Problems of Philosophy_, Cambridge, Harvard University Press, 1979.

_____, "A Suggestion About Mysticism," _Collected Essays and Reviews_, Ralph Barton Perry, ed., New York, Russell & Russell, 1969, p. 500-513.

_____, "Theology School Lectures, Religion After 1897," MS Box H, James Archives, Houghton Library, Harvard University, Cambridge.

_____, The Varieties of Religious Experience, Cambridge, Harvard University Press, 1985.

Jourard, Sidney M., "Growing Experience and the Experience of Growth," Chapter 13, Disclosing Man to Himself, New York, Van Nostrand Reinhold, 1968, p. 152-172.

Kelsey, Morton, Encounter With God: A Theology of Christian Experience, Minneapolis, Bethany Fellowship, 1972.

Kinast, Robert L., "Orthopraxis: Starting Point for Theology," Proceedings of the Catholic Theological Society of America, Vol. 38., 1983, p. 29-44.

Le Breton, Maurice, The Religion of William James, Cambridge, Harvard University Press, 1926.

Lee, James Michael, The Content of Religious Instruction: A Social Science Approach, Birmingham, Religious Education Press, 1985.

Linschoten, Hans, On the Way Toward a Phenomenological Psychology: The Psychology of William James, Pittsburgh, Duquesne University Press, 1968.

Maslow, Abraham H., Religions, Values, and Peak-Experiences, New York, Viking Press, 1970.

McDonnell, Kilian, O.S.B., "I Believe That I Might Experience," Theological Field Education: A Collection of Key Resources, Donald F. Beisswenger, Tjaard G. Hommes, and Doran McCarty, eds., The Association for Theological Field Education, 1981, p. 79-92.

Moran, Gabriel, F.S.C., Vision and Tactics: Toward an Adult Church, New York, Herder and Herder, 1968.

Nelson, C. Ellis, ed., Conscience: Theological and Psychological Perspectives, New York, Newman, 1973.

_____, "Theological Foundations for Religious Education," Changing Patterns of Religious Education, Marvin J. Taylor, ed., Nashville, Abingdon, 1984,

p. 10-22.

Niebuhr, Richard R., _Experiential Religion_, New York, Harper & Row, 1972.

Otto, Rudolf, _The Idea of the Holy_, John W. Harvey, trans., New York, Oxford University Press, 1958.

Perry, Ralph Barton, _The Thought and Character of William James_ (Briefer Version), New York, Harper Torchbooks, 1964.

_____, _The Thought and Character of William James_, Vol. I, Boston, Little, Brown, 1935.

_____, _The Thought and Character of William James_, Vol. II, Boston, Little, Brown, 1935.

Rizzuto, Ana-Maria, _The Birth of the Living God: A Psychoanalytic Study_, Chicago, University of Chicago Press, 1979.

Santayana, George, _Character and Opinion in the United States_, New York, Norton, 1967.

Schleiermacher, Friedrich, _The Christian Faith_, Second German Edition, H. R. Mackintosh and J. S. Stewart, trans., Edinburgh, Clark, 1928.

_____, _On Religion: Speeches to its Cultured Despisers_, Third German Edition, John Oman, trans., New York, Harper Torchbooks, 1958.

Schneiders, Sandra M., I.H.M., "The Contemporary Ministry of Spiritual Direction," _Chicago Studies_, Vol. 15, Spring 1976, p. 119-135.

Smet, Walter, S.J., "Religious Experience in Client-Centered Therapy," _The Human Person_, Magda B. Arnold and John A. Casson, S.J., eds., New York, Ronald Press, 1954, p. 539-547.

Stark, Rodney, "A Taxonomy of Religious Experience," _Journal for the Scientific Study of Religion_,

Vol. 5, No. 1, October 1965, p. 97-116.

Stevens, Richard, _James and Husserl: The Foundations of Meaning_, The Hague, Martinus Nijhoff, 1974.

Strunk, Orlo, Jr., _Mature Religion: A Psychological Study_, New York, Abingdon, 1965.

Tart, Charles T., _Altered States of Consciousness_, New York, Doubleday, 1972.

Thornton, Edward E., _Theology and Pastoral Counseling_, Englewood Cliffs, New Jersey, Prentice-Hall, 1964.

Tillich, Paul, _Systematic Theology_, Vol. I, New York, Harper & Row, 1967.

Tracy, James J., "Faith and Growth: A Psychology of Faith," _Insight_, Vol. 5, No. 3, Winter 1967, p. 15-22.

Westerhoff, John H., III, _Will Our Children Have Faith?_ New York, Seabury Press, 1983.

Wilshire, Bruce, _William James and Phenomenology: A Study of "The Principles of Psychology,"_ Bloomington, Indiana University Press, 1968.

About the Author

John J. Shea is Assistant Professor of Psychology and Pastoral Counseling in The Graduate School of Religion and Religious Education of Fordham University. He is a graduate of Villanova University (1964), Augustinian College (1968), Catholic University of America (1970), St. Paul University (1974), and the University of Ottawa (1980).

He taught at Merrimack College (1968-1972) and at St. Paul University (1974-1976). A Resident in Pastoral Counseling at the Texas Research Institute of Mental Sciences (1977-1978), he worked in Cincinnati with An Active Spirituality for the Global Community (1978-1981) and with the Archdiocesan Consultation Services, Inc. (1978-1981).

A Catholic priest and a member of the Augustinian Order, he is a Fellow in The American Association of Pastoral Counselors.